How to Cook *Everything*™

Easy Weekend Cooking

Other Books by Mark Bittman

How to Cook Everything™

How to Cook Everything™: Quick Cooking

How to Cook Everything™: Holiday Cooking

How to Cook Everything™: Vegetarian Cooking

How to Cook Everything™: The Basics

The Minimalist Cooks at Home

The Minimalist Cooks Dinner

The Minimalist Entertains

Fish: The Complete Guide to Buying and Cooking

Leafy Greens

With Jean-Georges Vongerichten:

Simple to Spectacular

Jean-Georges: Cooking at Home with a Four-Star Chef

How to Cook *Everything*™

Easy Weekend Cooking

Mark Bittman

Illustrations by Alan Witschonke

WILEY

Wiley Publishing, Inc.

Library of Congress Cataloging-in-Publication Data

Bittman, Mark.

  How to cook everything. Easy weekend cooking / Mark Bittman ;

illustrations by Alan Witschonke.— 1st ed.

    p. cm.

  ISBN 0-7645-2513-1 (Paperback : alk. paper)

  1. Entertaining. 2. Cookery. 3. Menus. I. Title: Easy weekend

cooking. II. Title.

  TX731.B47 2003

  642'.4—dc21

                    2003008736

Photos on pages xii, 14, 28, 44, 56, and 82 © PhotoDisc, Inc. / Getty Images
Photos on pages 70 and 100 by David Bishop

To my parents and my kids

WILEY PUBLISHING, INC.

Publisher: Natalie Chapman

Executive Editor: Anne Ficklen

Senior Editor: Linda Ingroia

Production Editor: Tammy Ahrens

Cover Design: Cecelia Diskin

Book Design: Edwin Kuo and Anthony Bagliani, Solid Design

Interior Layout: Nick Anderson

Manufacturing Buyer: Kevin Watt

Contents

Acknowledgments

I have been writing about food for nearly 25 years, and it's impossible to thank all the people who have helped me make a go of it during that time. Most of them know who they are—we have shared cooking, eating, and talking, much of what constitutes my life—and together I do owe them a broad "thanks."

However, some special friends and colleagues have been there for me and helped me out in recent years, and I want to thank them especially: Mitchell Orfuss, Naomi Glauberman, John Bancroft, Madeline Meacham, David Paskin, Pamela Hort, Jack Hitt, Semeon Tsalbins, Susan Moldow, Bill Shinker, Jim Nelson, Fred Zolna, Sherry Slade, Lisa Sanders, Genevieve Ko, Charlie Pinsky, Geof Drummond, Sam Sifton, Nancy Cobb, and Steve Rubin.

I have been blessed, too, with great colleagues at Wiley: Linda Ingroia, who has worked tirelessly on the new *How to Cook Everything*™ series; Edwin Kuo, Jeffrey Faust, Cecelia Diskin, and Holly Wittenberg for great covers and interiors; Tammy Ahrens, the production editor, and Christina Van Camp for keeping keen eyes on clarity and consistency; and Kate Fischer and Michele Sewell for managing *How to Cook Everything* publicity opportunities. Jennifer Feldman got the *How to Cook Everything* series up and running and Natalie Chapman and Robert Garber have given it tremendous support. My agent, Angela Miller, is simply the best and has been a terrific influence in my life for over a decade; huge thanks to her, as always.

Few of my cookbooks would have been written without the help and inspiration of Karen Baar, to whom I remain grateful. And, as always, special thanks to my fabulous children, Kate and Emma, and my most frequent companions, John H. Willoughby, John Ringwald, and Alisa X. Smith, all of whom give me invaluable love and perspective on a daily basis, and newfound confidence in the world of cooking.

How to Cook Everything™: Easy Weekend Cooking is a simple-to-use collection of my favorite recipes for leisurely weekend cooking. These are especially flavorful dishes that may take more time than I normally spend on busy weekdays but result in deliciously satisfying meals, those more suitable for entertaining friends or family. And this is restorative cooking, relaxing and unhurried.

Though you probably have more time and energy to cook on weekends than on weekdays, that doesn't mean you want to be in the kitchen all day, or to delve into super-complicated recipes that require the training of a chef. You may want to cook something special and elaborate for your family or other guests, whether you want the rich, slowly cooked dishes that counter winter's chill or the great taste, ease, and excitement of summer grilling.

This book offers both good recipes and sound overall techniques and strategies—in short, guidance—to help you make these meals. The recipes range from comfort foods like beef stew and baked beans, to special occasion dishes like lobster bisque and osso buco. Though in one way this book is a straightforward guide for specific meals, most of the dishes can be varied to your taste or diet, or what's available in your kitchen, so it can also be viewed as a springboard for your own creativity. To encourage that, I've included not only more than 90 recipes, but dozens of variations, tips to help you shop for, prepare, and cook the recipes, lists of flavoring ideas, and illustrations on some tricky techniques like debearding mussels and trimming artichokes.

If you're interested, and if it will help you plan your meals, many of the recipes here can also be made for weekdays. You may need to do a little extra shopping or prep in advance, but these simple recipes with special flavor don't have to be saved for special occasions. The easy weekend recipes and variations that also work for weekdays are labeled with a 🅦 symbol. Obviously, if you have enough time you can cook anything you like on a weekday; but these are recipes that are relatively fast, simple, and straightforward.

Finally, if you're looking for easy weekend meal ideas, you'll find 20 menus (pages 114 to 115) for family meals and impress-the-guests feasts.

When it comes to easy weekend cooking, I imagine your goals and mine are the same—to make good food for the people you want to spend special time with without getting too overwhelmed by cooking the meal. This book can help you do that.

What to Know About Easy Weekend Cooking

Weekends give you a great opportunity to cook and have fun at the same time. You can take a little more time to prepare food that really qualifies as magnificent; experiment with new cuisines, techniques, or your own inspirations; and create memorable meals—memorable for the experience of cooking really good food, memorable because the eating of it is such a joy, memorable because they bring people you care about together.

Presumably, this is all a labor of love. But there is no denying that forethought and a fair amount of work must go into creating great meals like this. And what make weekend cooking less stressful are the same principles that work for home cooks during the rest of the week: Keep your pantry well stocked; plan ahead; get others to help out with the shopping, preparation, cooking, and cleanup; and, most important, plan according to your abilities and your needs.

This is a time to make great meals, but still not a time to be overly ambitious; a three-course meal that makes everyone happy is far better than a larger one in which you become completely stressed out. If you're cooking to share great food with people you care about, you have to be able to enjoy it yourself.

Cooking Basics

Here are some thoughts and guidelines on efficient, safe, and smart cooking in general and on weekend cooking in particular.

Time

Time is always precious, but on the weekends you can afford to burn a little more of it. Still, it's worthwhile to think ahead. If you have the makings of a meal or two on hand at all times just by maintaining the right mix of staples, even if you want to invite friends over at the last minute, you will be ready.

Different people like to eat different ways, obviously, but certain foods belong in every kitchen all the time, and keep nearly indefinitely.

With this list alone you will be equipped to make literally dozens of different dishes, from salads to sweets. When you throw in the fresh ingredients that you're likely to have in the refrigerator as a result of special shopping jaunts—vegetables, herbs, fruit, meat, fish, milk, cream, cheese, and other perishables—the result is that you'll be able to prepare most of the more than 90 recipes in this book without going out to search for special ingredients.

In general, I consider whole, fresh ingredients a priority. Of course, when time is an issue, I am not against the use of store-bought stock, or frozen spinach, as part of a recipe, especially where the ordinary-at-best nature of such products is disguised by the other ingredients in the recipe. But I do not believe in "miracle" recipes based on canned or dried soups, artificial mayonnaise, or powdered desserts. Real cakes begin with flour and butter, and real whipped cream does not come from a can. This is a cookbook, not a chemistry class; to cook good dishes you must start with real food.

A word about timing. The timing for every recipe is always approximate. The rate at which food cooks is dependent on the moisture content and temperature of the food itself; measurements (which are rarely perfectly accurate); heat level (everyone's "medium-high" heat is not the same, and most ovens are off by at least 25 degrees in one direction or another); the kind of equipment (some pans conduct heat better than others); even the air temperature. So be sure to use time as a rough guideline, and judge doneness by touch, sight, and taste.

Food Safety

On the weekends, you might plan ambitious menus, so you cut corners to get everything ready in time, or you might cook with unfamiliar ingredients and don't think about food safety because you're learning about the new foods. However, most foodborne illnesses can be prevented, so it's worth taking precautions.

Keep your hands and all food preparation surfaces and utensils perfectly clean; soap and hot water are all you need. Wash cutting boards after using, and don't prepare food directly on your counters unless you wash them as well. Change sponges frequently too, and throw your sponges in the washing machine whenever you wash clothes in hot water. (Or microwave your sponge every day.) Change your kitchen towel frequently also—at least once a day.

It should go without saying that your refrigerator functions well (35°F is about right, and 40°F is too warm) and food should be stored in the refrigerator until just before cooking (or removed for no more than an hour before cooking if you wish to bring it to room temperature first) or whenever you're not using it. Your freezer should be at 0°F or lower. Thaw foods in the refrigerator, or under cold running water. And never place cooked food on a plate that previously held raw food.

Those are the easy parts, which everyone should do without question. The other parts—such as cooking food to the right temperature—are more difficult. Of common foods, cooked vegetables and grains are the safest; next comes cooked fish; then comes cooked meat other than hamburger; then comes cooked chicken, eggs, and hamburger, with which most concerns are associated. I don't advocate cooking all meats until they are well done (and inedible); but work with the tastes and doneness that you're comfortable with. I cook chicken to 165°F (measured, with an instant-read thermometer, in a couple of places in the thigh); this is lower than the USDA recommendations, but if the thermometer is accurate it's safe, and the bird is not hideously overcooked.

My overall strategy is that I keep a spotlessly clean kitchen, wash my hands about forty times a day, and cook food so that it tastes as good as it can; that's how the recipes in this book are designed.

Equipment

Every kitchen should have the right basic equipment (described fully in *How to Cook Everything*), but there are some things that are more useful for the kind of cooking we do on weekends. These include:

Carving knife: Not something you will use every day, but really handy for roasts and large birds.

Stockpot: Ultimately, the leftovers go here.

Large roasting pan: Like a lasagne pan, sturdy, with two handles, and (preferably) a non-stick surface.

Muffin tins: If people are staying or coming for breakfast or brunch.

Pie plates: You will probably need more than one; 9 inches is standard. A 10-inch springform pan (with a removable rim) is great for cheesecake.

Cake pans: If you love making cakes for company.

Instant-read thermometer: The most accurate way to determine whether food is done, especially for inexperienced cooks. You may never have cooked a turkey in your life, but when that thermometer reads 165°F, you know it's done.

Rolling pin: You can't make a pie crust without one. Buy a straight rolling pin without ball bearings; it's lighter, more easily maneuvered, and unbreakable.

Zester: The easiest way to remove zest from lemons and other citrus (but not the only way; you can remove zest with a vegetable peeler and mince it by hand.)

Food processor: Practically a necessity for large-scale cooking.

Electric mixer: If you bake a lot, you will want both a powerful standing mixer and a small, handheld mixer. If you bake occasionally, you will want either.

Blender (countertop; handheld or immersion blenders work for smaller jobs): For drinks and soups.

And if you want great grilling taste, you should of course have the following:

◆ gas or charcoal grill
◆ indoor grill or grill pan
◆ grill tongs, and grill cleaners

1 | Breakfast and Brunch

Ⓦ Weekday

Best Scrambled Eggs

A Sunday morning indulgence, these take cream, butter, tarragon, some time, and—the really hard part—some patience. Serve them with lots of toast. With thanks to James Beard.

Makes 2 servings

Time: 40 minutes

---

2 to 4 tablespoons butter

5 eggs

Salt and freshly ground black pepper to taste

1 teaspoon minced fresh tarragon leaves or 1/4 teaspoon dried tarragon

2 tablespoons cream

---

5 Additions to Scrambled Eggs

You can add almost anything to the beaten uncooked eggs before scrambling. Try these:

1 Chopped fresh herbs, 1 teaspoon (stronger herbs) to 1 tablespoon (milder ones). For scrambled eggs *aux fines herbes*, add about 1/2 teaspoon tarragon, 1 teaspoon chervil, and 1 tablespoon each parsley and chives, all chopped.

2 Minced pickled jalapeños to taste

3 Chopped roasted red peppers (see Marinated Roasted, Grilled, or Broiled Peppers, page 96, or jarred), up to 1/2 cup

4 Sautéed mushrooms or other cooked vegetables, cut into small dice, about 1/2 cup

5 Chopped salami or other smoked meats, about 1/2 cup

1 Place a medium skillet, preferably non-stick, over medium heat for about 1 minute. Add the butter and swirl it around the pan. After the butter melts, but before it foams, turn the heat to low.

2 Beat the eggs with the remaining ingredients and pour into the skillet. Cook over low heat, stirring occasionally with a wooden spoon. At first nothing will happen; after 10 minutes or so, the eggs will begin to form curds. Do not lose patience: Keep stirring, breaking up the curds as they form, until the mixture is a mass of soft curds. This will take 30 minutes or more. Serve immediately.

Baked Eggs with Spinach

This is a filling baked egg dish, sometimes called Eggs "Florentine," with the eggs cooked in individual nests of spinach. A great use for leftover spinach if you have it.

Makes 4 servings

Time: About 45 minutes

About 1½ pounds fresh spinach, washed and trimmed

3 tablespoons butter or olive oil

8 eggs

Salt and freshly ground black pepper to taste

½ cup freshly grated Parmesan cheese

½ cup plain bread crumbs

Toast or toasted English muffins

1 Preheat the oven to 350°F.

2 Bring a large pot of water to a boil; salt it. Place the spinach in the water and cook for about a minute, or until it is bright green and tender. Drain well. When it is cool enough to handle, squeeze the moisture from it and chop.

3 Place the butter or oil in a 9 × 13-inch baking pan and put the pan in the oven. When the butter melts or the oil is hot, toss the spinach in the pan, stirring to coat with the fat. Spread the spinach out and use the back of a spoon to make 8 little nests in the spinach. Crack 1 egg into each. Top with salt, pepper, cheese, and bread crumbs.

4 Bake for 15 to 20 minutes, or until the eggs are just set and the whites are solidified. Scoop out some spinach with each egg and serve on toast or toasted English muffins.

Ⓦ Spanish Potato Omelet

This egg pie is called *tortilla* in Spain. Wonderful at breakfast or brunch, but also perfect for a late supper or anytime snack, and therefore appropriate for weekday cooking; in fact, it makes the basis for a great quick dinner.

Makes at least 4 servings

Time: 45 minutes

⅓ cup extra-virgin olive oil

1 pound waxy red or white potatoes, peeled and cut into ⅛-inch-thick slices

Salt and freshly ground black pepper to taste

1 large onion, sliced

1 red bell pepper, stemmed, peeled if desired, seeded, and sliced

1 teaspoon minced garlic

6 eggs

½ cup minced fresh parsley leaves

1 Place about half the olive oil in a large ovenproof skillet, preferably non-stick, and turn the heat to medium. Add the potato slices and season liberally with salt and pepper. Cook, turning gently from time to time, until they soften, about 20 minutes. Remove with a slotted spoon.

2 Add the remaining oil to the pan, followed by the onion and red pepper, and cook, stirring occasionally, until nice and soft, about 10 minutes. Add the garlic and cook another 2 minutes. Preheat the oven to 375°F.

3 Return the potatoes to the skillet and turn the heat to medium-low. Continue to cook, turning with a spatula, for about 5 more minutes. Beat the eggs with the parsley.

4 Turn the heat to low and pour the eggs over the potatoes. Shake the pan to distribute the eggs evenly and cook, undisturbed, for about 5 minutes. Transfer to the oven and bake until the mixture is set, about 10 minutes more. Remove the pan and cool to room temperature before cutting into chunks or wedges; serve.

Breakfast Sausage

Most breakfast sausages have the characteristic flavor of sage—which you'll recognize immediately—and are almost as easy to make as hamburgers. Fatty ground pork can be combined with any spice mixture you like to make sausages, so try your favorite.

Makes about 2½ pounds, about 8 servings

Time: 30 minutes, including cooking time

2 pounds lean boneless pork

½ to ¾ pound fresh pork fatback (not salt pork)

1 teaspoon salt

½ teaspoon freshly ground black pepper

⅛ teaspoon freshly grated nutmeg

1 teaspoon minced fresh sage leaves or about ½ teaspoon dried sage, crumbled

1 Cut the pork and fat into 1-inch cubes. Place about 2 cups of the mixture into the container of a food processor and mince in 1-second pulses until finely chopped. Take your time and be careful not to pulverize the meat. As you finish each batch, transfer it to a bowl.

2 Season with the spices; add a little water if the mixture seems very dry. If you have time, break off a small piece, shape it into a patty, and cook it in a small skillet over medium heat until brown on both sides and cooked through. Taste it and adjust seasonings if necessary.

3 This amount will make 8 large sausages, so you might want to freeze half if you're serving only 4 people (shape the sausage before freezing it). Shape into patties. Heat a large skillet over medium heat for 2 or 3 minutes, then add the patties. Let them cook, undisturbed, for about 5 minutes, then move them so they brown evenly. When one side is brown, turn to brown the other. Serve when nicely browned and cooked through, about 15 minutes total.

Shopping Tip: The best sausage contains a good deal of fat—about 30 percent by weight of the amount of meat. The minimum I call for is 25 percent, but if you like, you can use less fat to a minimum of about 20 percent—a little more than 6 ounces. Less than that and you will have a hockey puck rather than a sausage (imagine a nearly all-lean hamburger cooked until well done, and you'll have a good sense of what I'm talking about).

Home-Fried Potatoes

Home fries have long been the domain of diners, but they're easy and fun to make at home. If you don't have marjoram, try these with oregano or parsley.

Makes 4 servings

Time: 45 minutes

1½ to 2 pounds waxy red or white potatoes, peeled and cut into ½-inch to 1-inch cubes

¼ cup butter or olive oil, more or less

1 teaspoon chopped fresh marjoram, or ½ teaspoon dried, optional

1 large onion, peeled and chopped

Salt and freshly ground black pepper to taste

1 Place the potatoes in a pot of salted water, bring to a boil, and simmer until nearly tender, 10 to 15 minutes. Drain well.

2 Heat the butter or oil over medium-high heat in a 12-inch non-stick skillet for 3 to 4 minutes. You can use more butter or oil (for crisper potatoes) or less (for less fat). Add the potatoes, marjoram, and onion and cook, tossing and stirring from time to time (not constantly), until the potatoes are nicely browned all over and the onion is softened and beginning to brown, 10 to 20 minutes. Taste and add salt and pepper as needed, then serve.

Ⓦ Overnight Waffles

Super-crisp outside, light and tender inside, with the complex flavor of yeast-risen batter, these are the best waffles you can make, and they're no more work than any other waffle; you just have to think ahead. One note: Eat waffles immediately or they get soggy. You can keep them warm on a rack in a 200°F oven for 5 minutes, but not much longer. I serve them as they come from the iron, for waffles are delicate creatures. If you like, serve with some melted butter and gently warmed maple syrup.

These can make a quick weekday breakfast, too, as long as you remember to start the batter the night before.

Makes 4 to 6 servings

Time: 8 hours, or more, largely unattended

½ teaspoon instant yeast

2 cups all-purpose flour

1 tablespoon sugar

½ teaspoon salt

2 cups milk

8 tablespoons (1 stick) butter, melted and cooled

½ teaspoon vanilla extract (optional)

Canola or other neutral oil for brushing on waffle iron

2 eggs

1 Before going to bed, combine the dry ingredients and stir in the milk, then the butter and vanilla. The mixture will be loose. Cover with plastic wrap and set aside overnight at room temperature.

2 When you are ready to make them, brush the waffle iron lightly with oil and preheat it. Separate the eggs and stir the yolks into the batter. Beat the whites until they hold soft peaks. Stir them gently into the batter.

3 Spread a ladleful or so of the batter onto the waffle iron. After 2 minutes, gently pull up on the top of the iron. If there is resistance, give it another minute or 2 longer. (It usually takes about 3 to 5 minutes.) Serve immediately or keep warm for a few minutes in a low oven.

Preparation Tip: The waffle iron should be hot, clean, and lightly oiled. Even some non-stick irons aren't non-stick. If your first waffles stick, next time try brushing or spraying the iron lightly with oil before turning it on. When it's preheated (most irons have indicator lights, which go off when the iron is ready), open it for a minute to let any oily smoke escape, close it until it becomes hot again, then start cooking.

Baking Tip: Don't underbake the waffles. The indicator light on many waffle irons goes on when they are still a bit underdone. They won't be crispy enough, so wait an extra minute or so after that happens.

Ⓦ Light and Fluffy Pancakes

These are ethereal, clouds of egg made into cakes; they also develop a very nice crust. Add more sugar if you'd like them sweet. Try some of the variations or ideas to jazz up breakfast.

Makes 4 servings

Time: 20 minutes

---

1 cup milk

4 eggs, separated

1 cup all-purpose flour

Dash salt

1 tablespoon sugar

1½ teaspoons baking powder

Butter or canola or other neutral oil as needed

1 Preheat a griddle or large skillet over medium-low heat while you make the batter.

2 Beat together the milk and egg yolks. Mix the dry ingredients. Beat the egg whites with a whisk or electric mixer until stiff but not dry.

3 Combine the dry ingredients and milk-yolk mixture, stirring to blend. Gently fold in the beaten egg whites; they should remain somewhat distinct in the batter.

4 Add about 1 teaspoon of butter or oil to the griddle or skillet and, when it is hot, add the batter by the heaping tablespoon, making sure to include some of the egg whites in each spoonful. Cook until lightly browned on the bottom, 3 to 5 minutes, then turn and cook until the second side is brown. Serve, or hold in a 200°F oven for up to 15 minutes.

Ⓦ **Blueberry Pancakes** Blueberries, about 1 cup, should be the last ingredient you add. If they are fresh, pick them over and wash and drain them well before adding. If they are frozen, add them without defrosting. Cook more slowly than you would plain pancakes, because they have a tendency to burn.

Ⓦ **Banana Pancakes** Really, really great, and a fine use for overripe bananas. Make the pancake batter as usual. After beginning to cook each batch, simply place a few rounds of ¼-inch-thick slices of banana directly onto the surface of the cooking batter; press them into each cake a little bit. Turn carefully and cook a little more slowly than you would plain pancakes, but be sure to cook through.

Ⓦ **Polenta Pancakes** Slowly add ½ cup cornmeal to 1 cup boiling water and cook over low heat, stirring, until smooth and well blended, about 3 minutes; cool. Make the batter as above and stir in the cornmeal mush before adding the beaten egg whites. You might also substitute molasses for the sugar in this variation, with excellent results.

Separating Eggs

Break the egg with the back of a knife or on the side of a small bowl.

The easiest way to separate eggs is to use the shell halves, moving the yolk back and forth once or twice so that the white falls into a bowl. Be careful, however, not to allow any of the yolk to mix in with the whites or they will not rise fully during beating.

5 More Ideas for Pancakes

1 Use the batter for Overnight Waffles, page 7.

2 Add chocolate chips as the pancakes are cooking (see Banana Pancakes, bottom left).

3 Add grated peeled apples or pears, crushed drained pineapple, or any other fruit, pitted, peeled, and chopped (or drained and chopped if canned), as you would blueberries. Or add peeled and sliced fresh fruit (or lightly cooked, for hard fruit such as apples) as you would bananas.

4 Add 1 tablespoon or more of freshly squeezed lemon juice to the batter, using baking soda ($1/2$ teaspoon per cup of flour) in place of baking powder. Add a little lemon rind as well if you like the flavor.

5 Use orange juice in place of milk; add 1 teaspoon grated or minced orange zest to the batter.

Muffins

Baking at home introduces you to one of life's great luxuries: fresh-from-the-oven muffins. Muffins are fast and easy to make and almost infinitely variable; when you make them yourself you can control the quality of ingredients and fat content. I don't like very sweet muffins, so I have kept the sugar to a minimum.

Makes 8 large or 12 medium muffins

Time: About 40 minutes

---

3 tablespoons melted butter or canola or other neutral oil, plus some for greasing the muffin tin

2 cups (about 9 ounces) all-purpose flour

¼ cup sugar, or to taste

½ teaspoon salt

3 teaspoons baking powder

1 egg

1 cup milk, plus more if needed

1 Preheat the oven to 400°F. Grease a standard 12-compartment muffin tin.

2 Mix together the dry ingredients in a bowl. Beat together the egg, milk, and butter or oil. Make a well in the center of the dry ingredients and pour the wet ingredients into it. Using a large spoon or rubber spatula, combine the ingredients swiftly, stirring and folding rather than beating, and stopping as soon as all the dry ingredients are moistened. The batter should be lumpy, not smooth, and thick but quite moist; add a little more milk or other liquid if necessary.

3 Spoon the batter into the muffin tins, filling them about two-thirds full and handling the batter as little as possible. (If you prefer bigger muffins, fill the cups almost to the top. Pour ¼ cup water into those cups left empty.) Bake 20 to 30 minutes, or until the muffins are nicely browned and a toothpick inserted into the center of one of them comes out clean. Remove from the oven and let rest for 5 minutes before taking them out of the tin. Serve warm.

Banana-Nut Muffins This is good with half bran or whole wheat flour. Add ½ cup roughly chopped walnuts, pecans, or cashews to the dry ingredients. Substitute 1 cup mashed very ripe banana for ¾ cup of the milk. Use honey or maple syrup in place of sugar if possible.

Blueberry or Cranberry Muffins Add 1 teaspoon ground cinnamon to the dry ingredients; increase sugar to ½ cup. Stir 1 cup fresh blueberries or cranberries into the batter at the last minute. You can also use frozen blueberries or cranberries here; do not defrost them first. Blueberry muffins are good with ½ teaspoon lemon zest added to the batter along with the wet ingredients. Cranberry muffins are excellent with ½ cup chopped nuts and/or 1 tablespoon minced orange zest added to the prepared batter.

ⓦ Cream Scones

Scones are no more than ultra-rich biscuits. You can make them with milk instead of cream, but that's missing the point. Note how quick they are to make; these are good any time.

Makes 10 or more scones

Time: 20 minutes

---

2 cups (about 9 ounces) all-purpose or cake flour, plus more as needed

1 scant teaspoon salt

4 teaspoons baking powder

2 tablespoons sugar

5 tablespoons cold butter

3 eggs

¾ cup heavy cream

⅓ cup dried currants or raisins

1 tablespoon water

---

4 Additions to Cream Scones

1 Stir ½ cup or more chopped nuts into the prepared batter.

2 Substitute chopped fresh fruit (apples, pears, peaches), whole berries (blueberries, cranberries), or minced dried fruit (figs, apricots) for the currants.

3 Add 1 teaspoon or more of ground cinnamon or ginger, or a pinch of nutmeg or allspice, to the dry ingredients.

4 Add ½ cup grated cheese along with the eggs and cream; reduce the sugar to 1 teaspoon and omit currants or raisins.

1 Preheat the oven to 450°F.

2 Mix the dry ingredients together in a bowl or food processor, reserving 1 tablespoon of the sugar. Cut the butter into bits and either pulse it in the food processor (the easiest) or pick up a bit of the dry ingredients, rub them with the butter between your fingers, and drop them again. All the butter should be thoroughly blended before proceeding.

3 Beat 2 of the eggs with the cream; with a few swift strokes, combine them with the dry ingredients. Use only a few strokes more to stir in the currants. Turn the dough out onto a lightly floured surface and knead it 10 times; no more. If it is very sticky, add a little flour, but very little; don't worry if it sticks a bit to your hands.

4 Press the dough into a ¾-inch-thick rectangle and cut into 2-inch rounds with a biscuit cutter or glass. Place the rounds on an ungreased baking sheet. Gently reshape the leftover dough and cut again; this recipe will produce 10 to 14 biscuits. Beat the remaining egg with 1 tablespoon of water, and brush the top of each scone; sprinkle each with a little of the remaining sugar.

5 Bake 7 to 9 minutes, or until the scones are a beautiful golden brown. These keep better than biscuits, but should still be eaten the same day you make them.

Sweet Rolls

This rich, sweet variation of bread, a nice option for brunch or a snack, is even better when made with one of the variations.

Makes about 24

Time: About 3½ hours, largely unattended

2½ cups (about 9 ounces) all-purpose flour, plus more as needed

1½ teaspoons instant yeast

½ teaspoon salt

⅓ cup sugar, plus more for sprinkling on rolls if desired

2 tablespoons butter, plus more for greasing the bowl and pan and for glazing

1 egg

½ cup milk, plus more as needed

Making Rolls

1

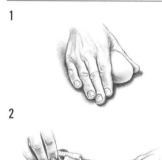

2

(Step 1) To make rolls, first roll a small lump of dough on a lightly floured surface until the seam is closed and smooth. **(Step 2)** Slash it with a sharp knife or razor before cooking.

1 Combine the flour, yeast, salt, and sugar in the container of a food processor fitted with the steel blade and process for 5 seconds. Add the 2 tablespoons butter and the egg and pulse a few times, until well combined. With the machine running, drizzle most of the milk through the feed tube. Process just until a dough ball forms; add more milk, 1 teaspoon at a time, if necessary. Knead by hand on a lightly floured surface for a minute or two longer, adding a little more flour or milk if necessary, until the dough is silky smooth and quite elastic.

2 Butter a bowl; place the dough in it. Cover and let rise until doubled in bulk, at least 2 hours. (You can hasten the process by placing it in a warm place.) Divide and shape into rolls (see illustration, bottom left); place on a greased baking sheet or in a buttered 12-compartment muffin tin. Cover and let rise until puffy, about 1 hour.

3 Preheat the oven to 400°F. Brush the tops of the rolls lightly with melted butter (you can also sprinkle them with a little sugar if you like) and bake until nicely browned, 20 to 30 minutes.

Cinnamon Rolls After the first rise, roll out the dough into a ½-inch-thick rectangle. Brush liberally with melted butter, then spread with a mixture of ½ cup sugar and 2 teaspoons ground cinnamon. If you like, dot it with about ¾ cup currants, raisins, chopped nuts, or a mixture. Roll it up, lengthwise, then cut into 1- to 1½-inch-thick slices. Place in a buttered 12-compartment muffin tin and let rise and bake as above. Brush with additional butter and sprinkle with sugar just before baking.

Caramel Rolls After the first rise, roll out the dough into a ½-inch-thick rectangle. Brush liberally with melted butter, then sprinkle with ½ cup brown sugar. If you like, dot it with about ¾ cup currants, raisins, chopped nuts, or a mixture. Roll it up, lengthwise, then cut into 1- to 1½-inch-thick slices. Place in a buttered 12-compartment muffin tin and let rise and bake as above. Brush with additional butter and sprinkle with sugar just before baking.

ⓦ Soft Fruit Shakes

Sitting on your kitchen counter is a tool that can turn any soft fruit into a great drink in moments: the blender. Use this as the basis for improvisation.

Makes 2 servings

Time: 15 minutes

---

2 cups cut-up mixed soft fruit: melons, skinned peaches, oranges, bananas, etc.

1 tablespoon freshly squeezed lemon juice, plus more if necessary

Sugar (preferably Sugar Syrup, at right), to taste

½ cup crushed ice

Combine all ingredients in a blender and whiz until smooth. Taste and adjust seasoning by adding more lemon juice or sugar syrup if necessary.

Preparation Tips: If you use berries in your fruit shake—especially raspberries and blackberries, but even strawberries—you may want to remove the seeds first. To do so, mash the berries in a bowl and then place them in a mesh strainer or sieve and press them with a wooden spoon or spatula to separate out the seeds.

Sweeten a shake with sugar only to taste; bananas, for example, can sweeten other fruit enough so that sugar isn't needed at all. Use Sugar Syrup if possible: You can make it in 10 minutes—see the recipe, below—and it keeps forever in the refrigerator. Alternatively, you may use honey, maple syrup, or any other sweetener.

For many fruits, you'll need some added liquid in the shake as well: Use orange, apple, grape, or pineapple juice, milk, or water (sparkling water adds a nice touch).

Sugar Syrup

Makes about 2 cups • Time: 10 minutes

The easiest all-purpose sweetener for any cold drink, including lemonade and iced tea, because it dissolves instantly. Make it in any quantity you like.

> **2 cups water**
> **2 cups sugar**

1 Combine in a small saucepan and turn the heat to medium.

2 Cook, stirring occasionally, until the sugar is completely dissolved. Store in the refrigerator.

2 | Salads and Soups

Ⓦ Weekday

Ⓦ Caesar Salad

The essentials in a great Caesar salad are garlic, egg, lemon juice, anchovies, and real Parmesan. Leave out any of these and you'll still have a good salad, but you won't have a great Caesar.

Makes 4 servings

Time: 20 minutes

---

1 clove garlic, cut in half

2 eggs, or substitute ½ cup pasteurized egg product

2 tablespoons freshly squeezed lemon juice

6 tablespoons extra-virgin olive oil

2 tablespoons minced anchovies, or to taste

Dash Worcestershire sauce

Salt and freshly ground black pepper to taste

1 large head romaine lettuce, trimmed, washed, dried, and torn into bits

Herb Croutons (page 22)

½ to 1 cup freshly grated Parmesan cheese

1 Rub the inside of your salad bowl with the garlic clove; discard it.

2 Bring a small pot of water to a boil. Pierce a tiny hole in the broad end of each of the eggs with a pin or a needle and boil them for 60 to 90 seconds; they will just begin to firm up. Crack them into the salad bowl, making sure to scoop out the white that clings to the shell.

3 Beat the eggs with a fork, gradually adding the lemon juice and then the olive oil, beating all the while.

4 Stir in the anchovies and the Worcestershire. Taste and add salt if needed and plenty of pepper. Toss well with the lettuce; top with the croutons and Parmesan, then bring to the table and toss again. Serve immediately.

Preparation Tip: Anchovies are part of the signature flavor of this dish. It doesn't taste fishy, though; the minced anchovies add a brininess to the seasoning, balancing the garlic, eggs, and cheese. You can leave them out of course, but also try adding only a little at first; you may find you like it.

W Salade Niçoise

Certain basics define salade Niçoise—tuna, tomatoes, anchovies, and, of course, greens. Hard-boiled eggs are also traditional, as are capers, olives, and onions, but can be omitted. Feel free to improvise—if you have fresh tuna, for example, grill it and use it. With some of the food precooked, and the judicious use of leftovers (you might have green beans from another meal, for example), this can serve as the centerpiece of a fast dinner.

Makes 4 to 6 servings

Time: About 45 minutes; far less if you prepare some ingredients in advance

½ pound green beans, trimmed

4 to 6 cups torn assorted lettuces and other salad greens (trimmed, washed, and dried)

2 cans Italian-style tuna in olive oil (preferred) or other tuna

2 Hard-Boiled Eggs (at right), peeled and cut into slices

1 cup good black olives (oil-cured are good for this)

3 ripe tomatoes, cored, seeded, and cut into quarters or eighths

1 bell pepper (any color but green), stemmed, peeled if desired, and cut into rings

6 anchovies (optional)

1 teaspoon capers (optional)

⅛ cup red wine vinegar, plus a little more if needed

About ½ cup extra-virgin olive oil

Salt and freshly ground black pepper to taste

1 small shallot, minced

1 teaspoon Dijon mustard

1 Steam the green beans (or poach them in boiling water to cover) for about 4 minutes. Drain, then dunk into ice water. Drain again.

2 Arrange all the salad ingredients nicely on a platter—greens on the bottom, topped, in separate sections, with tuna, egg slices, green beans, olives, tomatoes, and pepper, with the anchovies and capers sprinkled over all if you like. Or—less attractive but easier to serve—toss all the ingredients together.

3 Make the vinaigrette by adding the vinegar to the oil, along with the salt and pepper, shallot, and mustard. Stir and taste. Add more vinegar if necessary and adjust seasoning. Stir or shake vigorously, pour over the salad, and serve.

W Hard-Boiled Egg

Makes 1 serving per egg • Time: About 15 minutes

Much better when ever so slightly undercooked, so the yolk is on the creamy side.

1 Use a pin or needle to poke a hole in the broad end of each egg. Place each egg on a spoon, ladle, skimmer, or other tool and lower it into a small saucepan of gently boiling water; do not crowd.

2 Cook for 10 to 15 minutes; the shorter time guarantees a fully cooked white, and leaves some of the yolk a little underdone, which I prefer. Any time longer than 12 minutes will give you the standard hard-boiled egg (if you want to be doubly sure the egg is cooked through, increase the time to 15 minutes).

3 To remove the shell, plunge into cold running water for 30 seconds (if you want to eat the egg while hot) to 2 minutes (if you want to make shell removal as easy as possible and don't care whether the egg cools off). Remove the peel gently.

Ⓦ Grilled Chicken Salad

This is a great summer salad, when greens are abundant and you've got the grill going full time; definitely not just for weekends.

Makes 4 servings

Time: About 1 hour, including marinating time, plus time to preheat the grill

---

1 pound boneless skinless chicken breast, about 4 pieces, rinsed and patted dry with paper towels

¼ cup soy sauce

6 to 8 cups torn assorted salad greens (trimmed, washed, and dried)

Juice of 1 large lemon, plus more to taste

⅓ cup extra-virgin olive oil, approximately

1 teaspoon dark sesame oil

1 Start a charcoal or wood fire or preheat a gas grill or broiler; the fire should be quite hot and the rack about 2 inches from the heat source.

2 Pound the chicken lightly between 2 pieces of waxed paper so that it is of uniform thickness, less than ½ inch thick. Marinate the pieces in the soy sauce while the grill preheats.

3 Grill the chicken very quickly, on the hottest part of the grill; it should take no more than 2 to 3 minutes per side to become lightly browned.

4 Dress the greens with the lemon juice and olive oil, then cut up the chicken and scatter it over the salad. Sprinkle with the sesame oil. Taste and add more lemon juice if necessary, and serve.

Chicken or Duck Salad with Walnuts

You can make this rich dish with the meat of any bird, from turkey to partridge; the stronger the flavor, the better the dish.

Makes 4 servings

Time: Less than 30 minutes

---

1 tablespoon canola or other neutral oil

2 cups chopped raw boneless skinless chicken, duck, or other meat, preferably from the leg (chop the meat into ½-inch cubes), rinsed and patted dry with paper towels

2 tablespoons butter or olive oil

1 clove garlic, minced

½ cup walnuts or pecans, coarsely crumbled (do not chop)

¼ cup port, crème de cassis, or sweet sherry or wine

4 to 6 cups torn assorted salad greens (trimmed, washed, and dried)

About ½ cup Vinaigrette (at right)

A small handful minced fresh herb leaves, such as parsley or chervil, for garnish

1 Place the tablespoon of oil in a medium skillet and turn the heat to medium-high. A minute later, cook the meat in the oil, stirring, for about 2 minutes. Remove and set aside.

2 Wipe out the skillet and add the butter, still over medium-high heat; when the foam subsides, add the garlic and cook for 1 minute.

3 Add the walnuts and stir for 30 seconds. Add the wine and let it bubble out until the mixture is syrupy, stirring occasionally. Turn off the heat and return the meat to the pan to warm it up.

4 Dress the greens with the vinaigrette and toss; add more vinaigrette if necessary. Scatter the meat and nut mixture on top of the greens, garnish, and serve.

Ⓦ Vinaigrette

Makes 1 cup • Time: 5 minutes

Emulsified vinaigrettes are only important if you care. Sometimes that extra creaminess is nice (and an immersion blender works brilliantly). But usually it doesn't matter much; I just toss everything in a bowl and whisk it for 30 seconds or so.

¼ cup good vinegar, such as sherry, balsamic, or high-quality red or white wine, plus more to taste

½ teaspoon salt, plus more if needed

½ teaspoon Dijon mustard (optional)

¾ cup extra-virgin olive oil, plus more if needed

2 teaspoons minced shallots (optional)

Freshly ground black pepper to taste

1 Briefly mix the vinegar, salt, and optional mustard with an immersion blender, food processor, or blender, or with a fork or wire whisk.

2 Slowly add the oil in a stream (drop by drop if whisking) until an emulsion forms; or just whisk everything together briefly. Add the remaining oil faster, but still in a stream.

3 Taste to adjust salt and add more oil or vinegar if needed. Add the shallots and pepper. This is best made fresh but will keep, refrigerated, for a few days; bring back to room temperature before using.

This is a thin chicken soup—a warming but not super-filling first course—with the rice, meat, and vegetables acting as a garnish rather than a major player. Use orzo or other tiny pasta, angel hair or other thin noodles, ribbons or other egg noodles, or other cooked grains in place of the rice.

Makes 4 servings

Time: 30 minutes

---

5 to 6 cups Full-Flavored Chicken Stock (at right) or good quality store-bought chicken broth

½ cup long-grain rice or pasta

1 carrot, peeled and cut into thin slices

1 celery stalk, minced (optional)

1 cup raw or cooked chopped boneless skinless chicken, or more

Salt and freshly ground black pepper to taste

Minced fresh parsley or dill leaves for garnish

---

4 Additions to Chicken Soups

1 Spices, especially ginger, chiles, garlic, or other strong spices

2 Leftover chicken, grilled fresh chicken, small cubes of raw boneless chicken (which will cook in 2 minutes), or any other poultry

3 Small pieces of rind from Parmesan cheese, or grated cheese

4 Precooked vegetables of any type, as long as the flavor does not conflict with that of the soup. Onions, carrots, and celery are almost always appropriate.

1 Place the stock in a large, deep saucepan or casserole and turn the heat to medium-high. When it is just about boiling, turn the heat down to medium so that it bubbles but not too vigorously. Stir in the rice, carrot, and celery and cook, stirring occasionally, until they are all tender, about 20 minutes.

2 Stir in the chicken. If it is raw, cook another 5 to 8 minutes, until it is cooked. If it is cooked, cook 2 or 3 minutes, until it is hot. Season with salt and pepper, garnish, and serve.

Full-Flavored Chicken Stock

Makes 3 quarts • Time: 3 hours or more, largely unattended

This is a rich stock, the kind that will solidify when refrigerated. Don't use cooked, meatless chicken bones by themselves or the stock will lack a meaty flavor. But a combination of bones and meat, or raw, meaty bones alone, is fine. You can also include some precooked chicken in the mix.

3 to 4 pounds chicken parts and/or bones, rinsed and patted dry with paper towels

1 cup roughly chopped onion (don't bother to peel it)

1 cup roughly chopped carrot

½ cup roughly chopped celery

1 sprig fresh thyme or pinch dried thyme

½ bay leaf

Several sprigs fresh parsley

1 teaspoon salt, plus more if necessary

About 4 quarts water (16 cups)

1 Combine all ingredients in a stockpot.

2 Bring just about to a boil, then partially cover and adjust the heat so the mixture sends up a few bubbles at a time. Cook until the meat falls from the bones and the bones separate from one another, at least 2 hours.

3 Strain, pressing on the vegetables and meat to extract as much juice as possible. Taste and add salt if necessary.

4 Refrigerate, then skim any hardened fat from the surface. Refrigerate for 4 to 5 days (longer if you boil it every third day, which will keep it from spoiling), or freeze.

Chicken Soup with Cabbage and Thin Noodles

Chicken noodle soup, Chinese-style. Any soup will be better with homemade stock, but if you can't or don't want to make it, use low-sodium chicken broth and adapt seasoning as you cook. As long as you've got the stock, you can make this soup quite quickly.

Makes 4 servings

Time: 30 minutes

---

6 cups Full-Flavored Chicken Stock (at left) or good quality store-bought chicken broth

1 pound raw or cooked chopped boneless skinless chicken

1 pound bok choy or other cabbage, trimmed and washed

1 tablespoon peanut oil

1 teaspoon minced garlic

1 teaspoon peeled and minced fresh ginger

1 tablespoon soy sauce, plus more for serving

Salt to taste

8 ounces fresh (preferred) or dried thin Chinese egg noodles

1 Place the stock in a large, deep saucepan or casserole and turn the heat to medium-high. When it is just about boiling, turn the heat down to medium so that it bubbles but not too vigorously. If you are using raw chicken, cook it in the stock for about 2 minutes. Remove and set aside. If you are using cooked chicken, proceed to the next step.

2 Bring a large pot of water to a boil and salt it. Heat a wok or large skillet over medium-high heat. Cut the bok choy into 1- to 2-inch pieces, smaller for the stems, larger for the leaves. Add the peanut oil to the wok and cook the garlic and ginger, stirring, for 15 seconds, then add the bok choy. Raise the heat to high and stir-fry until the bok choy is fairly tender, 5 to 10 minutes. Add the soy sauce, taste for salt, and turn off the heat.

3 Cook the noodles in the boiling water until not quite tender; drain them. Add the noodles, cabbage, and chicken to the stock and cook until everything is heated through. Serve immediately.

Shopping Tip: Use fresh Chinese egg noodles without preservatives, which are especially common in egg noodles. Use fresh noodles within 2 to 3 days of buying them, or freeze them (defrost them in the refrigerator before cooking if possible).

Onion Soup

This onion soup has a thin coating of good cheese rather than the more common gobs of mozzarella or Cheddar. It's light but incredibly deep in flavor.

Makes 4 servings

Time: About 1 hour

---

4 tablespoons (½ stick) butter

4 large onions, thinly sliced (about 6 cups)

5 cups Full-Flavored Chicken Stock (page 20) or beef broth, preferably warmed

2 or 3 sprigs fresh thyme or pinch dried thyme

2 or 3 sprigs fresh parsley

Salt and freshly ground black pepper to taste

2 tablespoons cognac (optional)

4 Herb Croutons (at right), made with bread slices and butter

1 cup freshly grated Parmesan cheese

1 Melt the butter in a large, deep saucepan or casserole over medium heat. Add the onions and cook, stirring occasionally, until very soft and beginning to brown, 30 to 45 minutes.

2 Add the stock, turn the heat to medium-high, and bring just about to a boil. Turn down the heat so that the mixture sends up a few bubbles at a time. Add the seasoning herbs, salt, pepper, and cognac and cook for 15 minutes. Preheat the oven to 400°F. Fish out the parsley and thyme sprigs, if any. (You may prepare the soup in advance up to this point; cover and refrigerate for up to 2 days, then reheat before proceeding.)

3 Place a crouton in each of 4 ovenproof bowls. Add a portion of soup and top with cheese. Place the bowls in a roasting pan or on a sturdy baking sheet and bake for 10 minutes, or until the cheese melts. Serve immediately.

Herb Croutons

Makes about 2 cups cubes • Time: 10 to 15 minutes

A simple crouton, my favorite for soups and salads.

4 tablespoons extra-virgin olive oil, butter, or a combination

4 to 6 thick slices any bread, cut into cubes if you like

2 teaspoons or more minced fresh herbs: parsley, dill, chervil, thyme, or marjoram alone, or any mixture of fresh herbs you like

Salt to taste

1 Place the olive oil or butter in a large skillet and turn the heat to medium. When the oil is hot or the butter melts, add the bread cubes and cook, stirring, until brown all over.

2 Add the herbs and continue to cook for 1 minute more. Remove and sprinkle lightly with salt. Store in a covered container at room temperature for up to a week.

Potato Soup with Leeks

The simplest and most traditional of potato soups, at least in Western Europe, and still a delicious one. This is a soup you can build upon: Add cut-up turnips, diced tomatoes, carrots, or any other vegetables you like.

Makes 4 servings

Time: 30 minutes

---

2 large leeks

1 tablespoon butter or extra-virgin olive oil

3 medium potatoes, any type, peeled and cut into small cubes

Salt and freshly ground black pepper to taste

4 cups Full-Flavored Chicken Stock (page 20) or chicken, beef, or vegetable broth, preferably warmed

1   To prepare the leeks, first cut off all of the tough green leaves. Cut off the root end, then slice the leek lengthwise toward the root end but stop about 1/2 inch from the end. Fan out the leaves and rinse either under cold running water or in a bowl of cold water. Dry the leeks, then chop them.

2   Place the butter or oil in a large, deep saucepan or casserole and turn the heat to medium. When the butter melts or the oil is hot, add the vegetables. Season with salt and pepper and cook, stirring, for 2 or 3 minutes.

3   Add the stock and cook until the vegetables are very tender, about 20 minutes. (You may prepare the soup in advance up to this point. Cover, refrigerate for up to 2 days, and reheat before proceeding.) Adjust seasoning and serve.

Pureed Potato Soup with Leeks   Add 1/2 to 1 cup cream, milk, or half-and-half. Cool a bit, puree in a blender, then reheat. Adjust seasoning, garnish with minced chives, and serve.

Vichyssoise   Make above variation and chill thoroughly before garnishing with minced chives.

White Bean Soup with Greens and Rice

This is a hearty, vegetarian soup, but if you're interested in turning it into a big-time stew, see the variation below, which serves at least six.

Makes 4 to 6 servings

Time: About 1½ hours

½ pound dried white beans, washed and picked over (see Tips, below right)

1 teaspoon fresh thyme leaves or ½ teaspoon dried thyme

1 bay leaf

1 whole onion (don't bother to peel it)

½ pound kale, collard, or other dark greens

Salt and freshly ground black pepper to taste

5 cups chicken, beef, or vegetable stock, or water, warmed

1 cup rice

1 teaspoon minced garlic

1 Combine the beans, thyme, bay leaf, and onion in a large pot and cover with water. Bring to a boil and simmer until the beans are tender, adding water as necessary (use only enough water to cover the beans), about 1 hour. (You may prepare the soup in advance up to this point. Cover, refrigerate for up to 2 days, and reheat before proceeding.) While the beans are cooking, wash the greens well, then strip the leaves from the stem and reserve the stems. Roll the leaves up and slice them across the roll, then chop. Cut the stems into 1-inch or shorter lengths.

2 Remove the onion and bay leaf. Season the beans well and add the stock or water; bring to a boil and add the greens stems. Cook 2 minutes, then add the leaves and the rice and cook, stirring occasionally, until the rice is tender, about 15 minutes. Add a bit more water if necessary.

3 Stir in the garlic. Cook 1 minute, adjust the seasoning if necessary, and serve.

Preparation Tips: Beans are cleaned by machines, but spend a minute or two sorting through them just before soaking or cooking: Put the beans in a pot and fill it with water, then swish the whole thing around while looking into the pot. Remove beans that are discolored, shriveled, or broken and, obviously, remove any pebbles or other stray matter.

After sorting through the beans, dump them into a colander and rinse for another minute.

White Bean Soup with Greens, Rice, and Beef Cook the beans with 2 pounds short ribs or 1 to 1½ pounds brisket. When the beans are done, cut the meat into pieces, discarding the bones and fat, if any. Add 2 waxy, "new" potatoes, peeled and diced, along with the greens. Proceed as above, adding more stock or water if necessary. This is good with a teaspoon or two of vinegar added along with the garlic.

Ⓦ Pasta and Bean Soup

A warm, delicious classic—called *pasta e fagioli* or, in Italian-American lingo, *pasta fazool*—that can be varied in many ways but always contains two essential comfort foods at its heart.

Makes 6 servings

Time: 45 minutes to 1 hour with precooked beans

---

5 tablespoons extra-virgin olive oil

1 large onion, chopped

2 teaspoons minced garlic

2 sprigs fresh rosemary or 1 teaspoon dried rosemary

3 cups drained cooked kidney, cannellini, borlotti, or other beans or a mixture

2 cups cored, peeled, seeded, and diced tomatoes (canned are fine; include their juice)

6 to 8 cups chicken, beef, or vegetable stock or water, warmed

Salt and freshly ground black pepper to taste

½ pound tubettini or other small pasta (or larger pasta broken into bits)

½ cup minced fresh parsley leaves

½ cup freshly grated Parmesan cheese

1 Place 4 tablespoons of the olive oil in a large, deep saucepan or casserole and turn the heat to medium. A minute later, add the onion and half the garlic; cook until the onion softens, stirring occasionally, about 5 minutes.

2 Add the rosemary, beans, and tomatoes, and cook, stirring and mashing the tomatoes with your spoon, until the mixture is warm and the tomatoes begin to break down, about 10 minutes.

3 Add 6 cups of stock or water and a good amount of salt and pepper. Raise the heat to medium-high and bring to a boil. Turn the heat to medium-low and simmer for 10 minutes, stirring occasionally. (You may prepare the soup in advance up to this point. Cover, refrigerate for up to 2 days, and reheat before proceeding.)

4 Add the pasta, along with additional stock or water if necessary. Simmer until the pasta is nearly tender, 10 minutes or so. Add half the parsley and the remaining garlic and cook another 5 minutes, until the pasta is well done but not mushy.

5 Sprinkle with the remaining parsley and drizzle with the remaining olive oil. Serve, passing the cheese at the table.

Lobster Bisque

This is a relatively simple and quick lobster bisque, one that retains two critical qualities: big-time lobster flavor and a luxurious creaminess. It isn't difficult or especially time-consuming to make, but it is incredibly impressive.

Makes 4 servings

Time: 1 hour

---

4 tablespoons (1/2 stick) butter

1 medium onion, chopped

1 teaspoon minced garlic

1 medium carrot, peeled and chopped

1 bay leaf

3 sprigs fresh thyme or 1/2 teaspoon dried thyme

4 to 8 lobster bodies, cooked or uncooked, with as many other lobster shells as you can scavenge, plus coral, tomalley, and any stray bits of meat you might find

1 cup dry white wine

1 cup cored, peeled, seeded, and chopped tomatoes (canned are fine; don't bother to drain)

6 cups Full-Flavored Chicken Stock (page 20), store-bought chicken or fish stock, or strained liquid reserved from boiling lobsters

1 cup heavy cream

Salt and freshly ground black pepper to taste

Minced fresh parsley leaves for garnish

1 Place 2 tablespoons of the butter in a large, deep saucepan or casserole over medium heat. When it melts, add the onion, garlic, carrot, bay leaf, and thyme and cook, stirring, until the onion softens, 5 to 10 minutes.

2 Add the lobster bodies and, if they are uncooked, cook, stirring, until they turn red, about 10 minutes (if they're already cooked, cook, stirring, about 5 minutes).

3 Add the wine and tomatoes and turn the heat to medium-high. Bring to a boil, then turn the heat to low, cover, and cook for 10 minutes.

4 Add the stock, turn the heat to high, and bring back to a boil. Once again, turn the heat to low and cover; cook 20 minutes. Remove the bay leaf and thyme sprigs. Remove the lobster shells, crack them if necessary, and pick off any meat you find. Return the bits of meat to the soup (reserve any large pieces of meat you have for the final addition, below).

5 Pass the soup through a food mill or puree it in a blender. (You may prepare the soup in advance up to this point. Cover, refrigerate for up to 2 days, and reheat before proceeding.) Return the soup to the pot and bring to a boil. Add the remaining butter, in bits, until it melts. Add the cream and any bits of lobster meat and heat through. Season with salt and pepper, garnish, and serve.

Shopping Tip: There are two good ways to obtain lobster bodies—one is to save them from a lobster feast. The other is to get them from fish markets, which either give them away or charge only minimally.

Cotriade

A traditional stew of northern France and a close relative of New England fish chowder. You can omit the bacon and cook the onions in 1/4 cup olive oil if you prefer, and cut not only the fat but the cooking time significantly by doing so.

Makes 4 servings

Time: 1 hour

1/2 cup minced bacon

2 large onions, roughly chopped

About 1 pound baking potatoes, peeled and cut into small chunks

Salt and freshly ground black pepper to taste

1 teaspoon fresh thyme leaves or 1/2 teaspoon dried thyme

6 cups Full-Flavored Chicken Stock (page 20) or store-bought fish or chicken stock or broth, preferably warmed

About 2 pounds fillets or steaks of white fish, cut into chunks

Juice of 1 lemon

Minced fresh parsley leaves for garnish

1 Place the bacon in a large, deep saucepan or casserole and turn the heat to medium-high. Cook, stirring, until it is crisp, about 10 minutes. Remove with a slotted spoon and set aside.

2 Turn the heat to medium and cook the onions in the bacon fat, stirring, until softened, about 5 minutes. Add the potatoes and cook, stirring occasionally, until they are well mixed with the onions and covered with fat. Season with salt, pepper, and thyme; stir, then add the stock.

3 Cook over medium heat until the potatoes are just tender, about 15 minutes.

4 Add the fish and cook another 5 to 10 minutes, until the fish is opaque and tender but not falling apart. Add the lemon juice, ladle into bowls, garnish, and serve.

Shopping Tip: Cotriade is traditionally made with halibut or sole, two firm-fleshed fish of the North Atlantic and North Sea. Since our sole is completely different—it's much softer—I recommend you stick to halibut. Monkfish would also be good.

3 | Pasta and Grains

Ⓦ **Weekday**

Pasta with Porcini

If you're lucky enough to come across a pound of fresh porcini, this is the recipe to make. If not, try the variation, which combines dried porcini with fresh mushrooms for nearly comparable flavor. Both are delicious, unusual, and quick.

Makes about 4 servings

Time: 30 minutes

---

1 pound porcini (cèpes) or other fresh wild mushrooms

1/3 cup olive oil, plus 1 tablespoon

Salt and freshly ground black pepper to taste

2 tablespoons minced shallots or 1 tablespoon minced garlic

1 pound any long or cut pasta

1/2 cup Full-Flavored Chicken Stock (page 20), store-bought chicken, beef, or vegetable broth, or pasta cooking water

About 1/2 cup minced fresh parsley leaves, plus more for garnish

1 Bring a large pot of water to a boil.

2 Wipe the mushrooms clean, or rinse them quickly if they are very dirty. Trim them of any hard, tough spots and cut them into small chunks or slices.

3 Heat the 1/3 cup of oil in a medium-to-large skillet over medium heat for 1 minute. Add the mushrooms and season with salt and pepper. Raise the heat to medium-high and cook, stirring occasionally, until the mushrooms begin to brown, at least 10 minutes. Add the shallots or garlic, stir, and cook for another minute or two until the mushrooms are tender. Turn off the heat.

4 Salt the boiling water and cook the pasta until it is tender but firm. When it is almost done, add 1/2 cup of stock or cooking water to the mushrooms, turn the heat to low, and reheat gently. Drain the pasta, reserving a little more of the cooking water if you have no stock. Toss the pasta and the mushrooms together with the remaining tablespoon of olive oil; add a little more liquid if the dish seems dry. Stir in about 1/2 cup of parsley, and serve garnished with more parsley.

Shopping Tip: Porcini (cèpes) are meaty and spectacular mushrooms. Increasingly (but still not commonly) seen fresh in this country, they are always available dried, and worth keeping in your pantry. Buy dried porcini from a reputable dealer in quantities of at least an ounce at a time; the small packages of 1/8 ounce for $3 are among the world's greatest rip-offs.

Preparation Tip: To reconstitute dried mushrooms: Soak in hot water to cover for 10 to 15 minutes, or until soft. Change the water if they are not softening quickly enough, but reserve the soaking water for use in sauces, stocks, and stews (strain it first; it might be sandy). Trim the hard parts from the mushrooms and use as you would fresh.

Cooking Tip: There are times when the shape of pasta matters and times when it does not. Tiny morsels, for example, such as orzo, tubetti, and ditalini, are best in soups, because they fit on a spoon. Long pastas, like spaghetti and linguine, are best with sauces that don't have large chunks in them. Sauces with chunks should be served with bigger, tube-shaped pasta, such as penne, rigatoni, or ziti, or with shells and elbows. With a sauce like this one, which has a few chunks but is also fairly juicy, you can use any pasta you like.

W Linguine with Dried Porcini In Step 2, prepare a pound of fresh domesticated mushrooms—button, cremini, shiitake, oyster, or a combination—as directed at the left. Soak at least 1/4 cup of dried porcini in hot water to cover for about 10 minutes, or until softened. Drain the porcini and squeeze out excess moisture, reserving the soaking liquid. Cut the porcini into bits and cook them with the fresh mushrooms and shallots or garlic, as in the master recipe. Follow the steps to the left, using the mushroom soaking liquid to augment or replace stock or pasta cooking water.

20 Best Recipes for Entertaining

These impressive but comforting foods are flavorful enough to earn raves, but not so fussy that they need any explanation.

Ⓦ Pasta with Provençal Seafood Sauce

You can use this basil-scented sauce as a base for almost any seafood you like, from squid and/or clams to conch and/or cod. Just be careful not to overcook the fish.

Makes at least 4 servings

Time: 40 minutes

---

1 tablespoon olive oil

½ cup diced onion

1 teaspoon minced garlic

½ teaspoon crushed red pepper flakes, or to taste

½ cup dry white wine

2 cups canned crushed tomatoes, not drained

1 pound linguine or cut pasta such as penne

¼ cup minced fresh parsley leaves

½ cup shredded fresh basil leaves

1 teaspoon fennel seeds

1 tablespoon minced lemon or orange zest

Salt and freshly ground black pepper to taste

½ pound medium-to-large shrimp (between 15 to 30 shrimp per pound), peeled, cut up if very large

½ pound sea scallops, cut in half if very large

1 Bring a large pot of water to a boil.

2 Put the oil in another large, deep pot over medium heat. One minute later, add the onion and cook, stirring, for 2 to 3 minutes. Add the garlic and cook for 1 minute. Add the red pepper flakes, wine, and tomatoes, bring to a boil, reduce the heat to medium-low, and let cook for about 15 minutes. (This sauce may be covered and refrigerated for a day or two, or put in a closed container and frozen for several weeks. Reheat before adding the seafood.)

3 Salt the boiling water and cook the pasta until it is tender but firm. When the pasta is almost done, add the parsley, half the basil, and all remaining ingredients to the sauce; simmer until the seafood is cooked through, 5 to 10 minutes.

4 Drain the pasta and serve with the sauce, garnished with the remaining basil.

Baked Ziti with Radicchio and Gorgonzola

Another dish showcasing the super flavor of Gorgonzola. Be careful not to cook the pasta to complete doneness; you should remove it from the cooking water when it is still so firm that you wouldn't want to eat it. It softens as the dish bakes.

Makes 4 servings

Time: About 1 hour

1 pound ziti, penne, or other cut pasta

2 small heads radicchio, about ½ pound, shredded

4 scallions, trimmed and very thinly sliced

2 cups milk, half-and-half, or cream

1 cup Gorgonzola, crumbled

1 cup freshly grated Parmesan cheese

Salt and freshly ground black pepper to taste

Butter for greasing the baking pan

½ cup plain bread crumbs, preferably fresh

1 Bring a large pot of water to a boil. Preheat the oven to 375°F.

2 Salt the boiling water and cook the pasta until it is barely tender, with a fairly chalky interior. Drain it well.

3 Mix the pasta with the radicchio, scallions, milk, Gorgonzola, and half the Parmesan. Taste for salt (it may not need any) and add pepper to taste.

4 Grease a 9 × 13-inch baking pan with butter and pour in the pasta mixture. Mix together the bread crumbs and remaining Parmesan and spread this on top of the pasta. Bake for about 30 minutes, until the mixture is hot and bubbly, then raise the heat to 450°F and continue to bake until the bread crumb mixture browns nicely, another 10 minutes or so. You can let this rest for 10 or 15 minutes before serving if you like.

Andrea's Pasta with Ribs

One of my favorite pasta recipes, a Neapolitan specialty that can make just a few ribs go a long way. As is usually the case, the ribs are best cooked slowly, to make them completely tender. If you take the time for this, you'll get ribs with delicious meat that comes off the bone with just a little tug; the rich flavor of the sauce is unbelievable.

Makes 4 servings

Time: 1½ hours

2 tablespoons olive oil

2 small dried hot red chiles (optional)

3 cloves garlic, chopped

6 to 8 meaty spare ribs, separated

Salt and freshly ground black pepper to taste

1 (28-ounce) can whole plum tomatoes, with their juice

1 pound ziti, penne, or other cut pasta

Freshly grated pecorino-Romano cheese (optional)

1 Warm the olive oil in a deep, broad saucepan over medium heat. After a minute, add the chiles, if you are using them, and garlic and cook, stirring, for about 30 seconds. Add the ribs and raise the heat to medium-high; cook, stirring occasionally, until the ribs have browned and given off some of their fat, about 10 to 15 minutes. Sprinkle with salt and pepper, crush the tomatoes with a fork or your hands, and add them to the pot with their juice.

2 Turn the heat to medium or medium-low—enough to maintain a nice steady bubbling, but nothing violent. Cook, stirring occasionally, until the ribs are very tender, nearly falling off the bone, about 1 hour. Remove the chiles from the sauce, if you have used them.

3 Bring a large pot of water to a boil. Salt the boiling water and cook the pasta until it is tender but firm. Drain it and sauce it; serve a rib or two to each diner along with the pasta. Pass the grated cheese at the table if you like.

Shopping Tip: Any pork ribs will work nicely here; standard spareribs are great, as are the leaner (and more expensive) baby back ribs, which are cut from the loin. Country ribs are not ribs at all but a section of the loin cut into rib-like chops; they'd be fine in this recipe also.

Gnocchi with Garlic and Oil

Gnocchi are dumplings—usually made with potatoes—served as if they were pasta. They're best when made fresh. Use baking ("Russet" or "Idaho") potatoes, not waxy potatoes. You can serve these with any tomato sauce or with butter and Parmesan.

Makes 4 first-course or 2 main-course servings

Time: 1 hour, or a little more

---

1 pound baking potatoes, whole, unpeeled

Salt and freshly ground black pepper to taste

About 1 cup flour

1/3 cup extra virgin olive oil, or a little more

1 tablespoon minced garlic

1/4 cup minced parsley leaves for garnish

Making Gnocchi

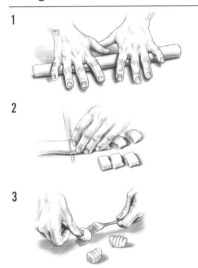

(Step 1) Roll a piece of the dough into a log. Use flour as necessary, but keep it to a minimum. **(Step 2)** Cut the dough into about 1-inch lengths. **(Step 3)** Roll each of the pieces off the back of the fork to form ridges.

1 Wash the potatoes and put them in a pot with salted water to cover. Cook until they are very tender, 30 to 45 minutes.

2 Drain the potatoes and peel them while they are hot (use a pot holder to hold them). Put them through a ricer, or mash them with a fork or potato masher; do not use a food mill or food processor. Place the riced potatoes in a bowl and season with salt and pepper. Bring a large pot of water to a boil and salt it.

3 Stir about 1/2 cup of flour into the bowl with the potatoes, and keep adding flour until the mixture forms an easy-to-handle dough. The amount of flour you add will depend on the potatoes. Not enough flour will make gnocchi that fall apart; more will make them firm and light; too much will rob them of flavor. Knead for a minute or so on a lightly floured surface. If this is the first time you have made gnocchi, pinch off a piece of the dough and boil it to make sure it will hold its shape; if it does not, knead in a bit more flour.

4 Break off a piece of the dough and roll into a rope about 1/2 inch thick. Cut the rope into 3/4- to 1-inch lengths; if you like, roll each of the pieces off the tines of a fork (see illustrations, at left) to score and curve it slightly. As you finish, place the gnocchi on a piece of waxed paper or a lightly floured baking sheet or similar surface, in one layer.

5 Put the oil in a small saucepan and turn the heat to low; add the garlic and cook until it bubbles. Turn the heat to a minimum and keep warm (if at any point the garlic begins to brown, turn off the heat).

6 Gently transfer the gnocchi to the boiling water, a few at a time. Stir gently. The gnocchi are done about a minute after they rise to the surface, which will happen very quickly; remove them with a slotted spoon as they finish cooking. Toss with the oil and garlic, garnish with the parsley, and serve.

Classic Lasagne, Italian-American-Style

Delicious comfort food that always impresses people. Spinach lasagne noodles are lovely to try, but you can of course use plain pasta or any flavor you like here.

Makes about 6 servings

Time: 45 minutes (with premade sauce)

At least 5 quarts water

12 fresh or dried lasagne noodles

2 tablespoons softened butter (preferred) or extra-virgin olive oil

3 cups ricotta cheese

3 cups, more or less, Meat Sauce (at right)

1½ cups freshly grated Parmesan cheese

1 pound grated mozzarella (preferably fresh)

Freshly ground black pepper to taste

Salt, if needed

1 Set at least 5 quarts of water in a large pot over high heat. When it comes to a boil, salt it.

2 Meanwhile, if you are using fresh pasta, cut the noodles so that they will fit reasonably snugly into your pan, about 13 inches long for a 9 × 13-inch pan.

3 Cook the noodles a few at a time; keep them underdone (if they are fresh, this means little more than a minute of cooking time). Drain carefully in a colander, then allow to rest on towels. Preheat the oven to 400°F.

4 Smear the bottom of your baking pan with the butter or oil, then place a layer of noodles, touching but not overlapping. Trim any overhanging edges. Cover the noodles with about 1 cup of the ricotta (thinned if necessary with some of the sauce), one-quarter each of the meat sauce, Parmesan, and grated mozzarella, then finish with a light sprinkling of black pepper. Between the meat sauce and the Parmesan, there should be enough salt, but if you feel it is underseasoned, add a little salt to each layer also. Make 4 layers (omitting the ricotta from the top layer), ending with a sprinkling of Parmesan. (The dish can be prepared in advance up to this point, then well wrapped and refrigerated for a day or frozen for a month; defrost in the refrigerator for a day before cooking if possible.)

5 Bake for about 20 to 30 minutes, until the lasagne is bubbly. Remove from the oven and let rest for 5 minutes before cutting and serving. Or let cool completely, cover well, and refrigerate for up to 2 days, or freeze for up to a month.

Meat Sauce

Makes a little more than 1 quart, enough for about 3 pounds of pasta • Time: Several hours, largely unattended

Ragù—as this sauce is called—is perfect for fresh pasta, or lasagne. Although the sauce doesn't require much work, it does require some attention over the course of a morning or afternoon. Double or triple the recipe if you like and freeze it in one-half pint or pint containers.

2 tablespoons olive oil

1 small onion, minced

1 carrot, peeled and minced

1 celery stalk, minced

¼ cup minced bacon or pancetta

½ pound lean ground pork (or use all beef)

½ pound lean ground beef

¾ cup dry white wine (or juice from the tomatoes)

1 (28- or 35-ounce) can whole plum tomatoes, drained (reserve juice, if needed instead of wine)

1 cup Full-Flavored Chicken Stock (page 20) or store-bought beef or chicken broth

Salt and freshly ground black pepper to taste

1 cup cream, half-and-half, or milk

Freshly grated Parmesan cheese (optional)

1 Put the olive oil in a large, deep skillet or saucepan. Turn the heat to medium-low and, a minute later, add the onion, carrot, celery, and bacon or pancetta. Cook, stirring occasionally, until the vegetables are tender, about 10 minutes.

2 Add the ground meat and cook, stirring and breaking up any clumps, until all traces of red are gone, about 5 minutes. Add the wine or tomato juice, raise the heat a bit, and cook, stirring occasionally, until most of the liquid is evaporated, about 5 minutes.

3 Crush the tomatoes with a fork or your hands and add them to the pot; stir, then add the stock. Turn the heat to low and cook at a slow simmer, stirring occasionally and breaking up the tomatoes and any clumps of meat that remain. After an hour or so, add salt and pepper. Cook for at least another hour, until much of the liquid has evaporated and the sauce is very thick. (This sauce may be covered and refrigerated for a day or two, or put in a closed container and frozen for several weeks. Reheat before completing.)

4 Add the cream, half-and-half, or milk and cook for another 15 to 30 minutes, stirring occasionally; taste and add more salt and/or pepper as needed. Serve immediately with any dried or fresh pasta, passing grated Parmesan, if you like, at the table.

This is an almost assaultive noodle dish, one in which heat—accented by vinegar and only slightly moderated by sugar and basil—should dominate. I like to make it mildly hot, then pass crushed red chiles at the table for those with cast-iron palates. Though it's special enough for company, this has become a weekday staple in my house.

Makes about 4 servings

Time: About 45 minutes, including time to soak the noodles

---

12 ounces rice noodles (fettuccine-width)

2 tablespoons peanut (preferred) or other oil

1 tablespoon minced garlic

5 small dried hot red chiles, or to taste

1/3 to 1/2 pound ground pork (preferred) or other ground meat, such as beef or turkey

1 tablespoon soy sauce and 2 tablespoons fish sauce (nam pla or nuoc mam, available at Asian markets), or a combination of either

1 tablespoon sugar

2 tablespoons rice (preferred) or other vinegar

1 cup shredded fresh basil leaves

Salt, if necessary

Crushed red pepper flakes (optional)

1 Soak the noodles in warm water to cover until soft; this will take from 15 to 30 minutes. You can change the water once or twice to hasten the process slightly, or you can simply cook the noodles as you would any other, taking care not to overcook. Drain thoroughly, then toss with half the oil.

2 Heat the remaining oil over medium-high heat in a wok or large, deep non-stick skillet for a minute or so, until the first wisp of smoke appears. Add the garlic and chiles and cook, stirring, for a minute. Add the meat and turn the heat to medium. Cook, stirring and mashing with a wooden spoon to break up clumps.

3 When almost all traces of red or pink disappear, add the soy and/or fish sauces and the sugar; stir to mix. Add the drained noodles and toss and stir to combine. Add the vinegar and most of the basil. Stir and taste; add salt if necessary. Serve, garnished with the remaining basil and passing the crushed pepper on the side.

Shopping Tip: Nam pla—Thai fish sauce, called *nuoc mam* in Vietnam—is little more than fish, salt, and water, an ancient way of preserving fish and adding its flavor to foods long after the catch is made. It's strong-flavored (and even stronger-smelling) but a great and distinctive substitute for soy sauce.

W Vegetarian Rice Noodles In Step 2, add 1 teaspoon peeled and minced fresh ginger along with the garlic and chiles. Cook 1/2 cup trimmed scallions, cut into 1-inch lengths, and 1/2 cup roughly chopped red bell pepper after the initial cooking of the garlic and chiles. Substitute 1 cup pressed or frozen tofu, diced, or 1 cup chopped seitan (processed wheat gluten, available at Asian markets) for the meat.

Broiled Polenta with Parmesan

This recipe—called *polenta crostini* in Italian—and its variation are great ways to enjoy polenta that has been cooked in advance.

Makes 4 servings

Time: At least 2 hours, largely unattended

---

1 teaspoon butter

1 recipe Polenta (at right), made with 3½ cups water and butter, Parmesan cheese, and herb

About ¼ cup freshly grated Parmesan cheese

1 Smear the teaspoon of butter in a thin layer on a baking sheet or on an 11 × 17-inch jelly-roll pan. Pour and spoon the cooked polenta onto the sheet. Work quickly, so the polenta doesn't stiffen.

2 When the polenta is cool enough to handle, cover it with a sheet of plastic wrap or waxed paper. Use your hands to flatten it to a thickness of about ½ inch all over. Refrigerate it until it is thoroughly cooled, at least 1 hour or overnight.

3 When you're ready to cook, preheat the broiler. Cut the polenta into serving-sized pieces, right on the baking sheet. Sprinkle with Parmesan and run under the broiler until heated through and lightly browned, 5 to 10 minutes. Serve immediately.

Ⓦ Polenta

Makes 4 servings • Time: About 30 minutes

Adding plenty of butter and cheese at the end of cooking helps make polenta richer. You could make this dish on a weekday, but it will require your full attention.

1 teaspoon salt, plus more if necessary

1 cup medium-grind cornmeal

Freshly ground black pepper to taste

2 tablespoons butter (optional)

¼ cup or more freshly grated Parmesan or crumbled Gorgonzola cheese (optional)

Snipped fresh chives or dill or minced fresh parsley leaves for garnish

1 Bring 4 cups water to a boil in a heavy medium pot, preferably non-stick; salt it and turn the heat to medium. Add the cornmeal a little at a time, whisking constantly with a whisk. Once you've whisked in all of the cornmeal, turn heat to low.

2 Cook, whisking every minute for the first 5 minutes, then switching to a flat-bottomed wooden spoon. Stir frequently, almost constantly, until all the water is absorbed. Soft polenta should be creamy; firmer polenta, such as that needed for slicing and grilling, or for the recipe at left, should begin to pull away from the sides of the pot. This will take about 15 minutes with the minimum amount of water and 30 to 40 with the maximum. Turn off the heat; taste and add more salt if necessary, along with some pepper.

3 Stir in the optional butter and cheese and stir until they dissolve. Garnish and serve immediately, passing more cheese at the table, if you like.

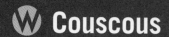

Couscous

All couscous, even that which is not labeled "instant," cooks quickly, so preparation time is minimal. For best results, use this technique even if you buy a box of couscous that gives different directions.

Makes 4 servings

Time: About 15 minutes

3 tablespoons butter

1½ cups couscous

2¼ cups Full-Flavored Chicken Stock (page 20) or store-bought chicken, beef, or vegetable broth, warmed

½ teaspoon salt, plus more if necessary

Freshly ground black pepper to taste

Minced fresh parsley leaves for garnish

1 Place 2 tablespoons butter in a medium saucepan and turn the heat to medium-low. When it melts, add the couscous and cook, stirring, until it is coated with butter, about 1 minute.

2 Add the stock all at once, along with ½ teaspoon salt. Bring to a boil, then turn the heat down to its minimum. Cover and cook until all the liquid is absorbed, 5 to 8 minutes.

3 Pour the couscous into a large serving bowl and stir in the remaining tablespoon butter with a fork, fluffing the couscous and breaking up any lumps. Add pepper and more salt if necessary, garnish, and serve.

Preparation Tip: To give couscous real flavor—because it doesn't have a lot of flavor on its own—serve couscous with any moist stew or other dish with plenty of gravy, like Classic Osso Buco (page 75) or Lamb Stew with Potatoes (page 78).

Persian Rice with Potatoes

You must use precooked rice for this dish—that way the potatoes become crisp rather than soggy—and it's best to use rice that has been cooked by the pasta-like method described in Precooked Grains (below).

Other than that, the only "secret" is to use a pot with a very tight-fitting lid.

Makes 4 servings

Time: At least 1 hour with precooked rice

---

8 tablespoons (1 stick) butter, plus
1 tablespoon

2 large potatoes, peeled and thinly sliced

1 medium onion, thinly sliced

2 cups cooked rice, slightly undercooked,
rinsed, and drained

Salt and freshly ground black pepper
to taste

½ cup blanched slivered almonds

1 Melt all but the 1 tablespoon of butter in a small saucepan. Use a little of it to film the bottom of a medium saucepan or casserole with a heavy, tight-fitting lid. Arrange the potato slices to completely cover the bottom of the casserole. Top with the onion and a thin layer of rice. Drizzle about half the melted butter over this and season with salt and pepper.

2 Pile on the rest of the rice and drizzle on the remaining melted butter. Season with salt and pepper. Put the top on the casserole and place over low heat. Cook, undisturbed, for about an hour.

3 Ten minutes before the dish is finished, melt the remaining butter in a small skillet over medium heat. Add the almonds and cook, stirring, until very lightly browned, about 5 minutes.

4 Stir the almonds into the rice without disturbing the bottom layer. To serve, scoop up some of the rice, then dig to the bottom of the casserole and scrape out some of the potatoes, which should be nicely browned.

Ⓦ Precooked Grains

Makes 4 servings • Time: 10 minutes to more than 1 hour, depending on the grain

---

At least 6 cups water

1½ cups white or brown rice, barley, wheat berries, or any other grain, rinsed

1 Bring at least 6 cups water to a boil in a medium-to-large pot; salt it. Stir in the grain and adjust the heat so that the water boils, but not furiously.

2 Cook, stirring occasionally, until the grain is tender. This will take about 7 or 8 minutes with some white rice, and as long as 1 hour or more for some brown rice, unpearled barley, wheat berries, and other unhulled grains. Add additional boiling water if necessary to keep grains covered.

3 Pour the grain into a strainer; plunge the strainer into ice-cold water to stop the cooking. Drain again. Reheat within 1 hour or refrigerate for later use.

W Pilaf with Indian Spices

To make this a whole-meal dish, add some boneless chicken pieces—from 1 to 2 cups total, cut into 1-inch or smaller chunks—along with the stock, and increase the spices by half.

Makes 4 servings

Time: About 30 minutes

A few threads of saffron or 1 teaspoon ground turmeric

2¹/₂ cups Full-Flavored Chicken Stock (page 20), store-bought chicken, beef, or vegetable broth, or water, heated to the boiling point

2 tablespoons butter or oil

6 cardamom pods or 2 teaspoons ground cardamom

Pinch ground cloves

¹/₂ cinnamon stick or ¹/₂ teaspoon ground cinnamon

1 bay leaf

1 cup chopped onion

1 tablespoon peeled and minced or grated fresh ginger or 1 teaspoon ground ginger

1¹/₂ cups long-grain rice, preferably basmati

Salt and freshly ground black pepper

Minced cilantro leaves for garnish

1 If you're using saffron, put it in the stock.

2 Place the butter or oil in a large, deep skillet which can later be covered and turn the heat to medium-high. When the butter melts or the oil is hot, turn the heat down to medium and add the cardamom, cloves, cinnamon, bay leaf, and turmeric if you are using it. Cook, stirring very frequently, until the spices are fragrant, about 2 minutes.

3 Add the onion and ginger and cook, stirring, until the onion softens, about 5 minutes. Add the rice all at once, turn the heat to medium, and stir until the rice is glossy and coated with oil or butter, 2 or 3 minutes. Season well, turn the heat down to low, and add the liquid, all at once. Cover.

4 Cook for 15 minutes, then check the rice. When it is tender and the liquid absorbed, it's done. If not, cook for 2 or 3 minutes and check again. Remove the cinnamon stick and the bay leaf, garnish, and serve.

Shopping Tip: In most homes, spices like cardamom do not get used frequently enough to be replaced often, so it's best to buy whole spices, which keep far longer than the preground variety. Cardamom pods can be used whole; pick them out before serving (or warn your guests to pick them out before eating).

Ⓦ Risotto with Vegetables

You can make this delicious dish, even when it seems you have nothing in the house. Of course, if you have more vegetables, use them; just make sure to cook them until just soft before adding the rice and liquid.

Makes 4 to 6 servings

Time: 45 minutes

---

4 to 6 cups Full-Flavored Chicken Stock (page 20), store-bought chicken, beef, or vegetable broth, or water

2 tablespoons butter or extra-virgin olive oil, plus 2 tablespoons butter, softened (optional)

1 medium onion, minced

1 celery stalk, minced

1 medium carrot, peeled and minced

1½ cups arborio or other short-grain rice

Salt and freshly ground black pepper to taste

½ cup dry white wine

½ cup fresh or frozen and thawed peas

Freshly grated Parmesan cheese

1 Warm the stock over medium heat. Place the butter or oil in a large saucepan or skillet, preferably non-stick, and turn the heat to medium. When it's hot, add the onion, celery, and carrot and cook, stirring occasionally, until the onion softens, 3 to 5 minutes.

2 Add the rice and stir until it is coated with butter. Add a little salt and pepper, then the white wine. Stir and let the liquid bubble away.

3 Begin to add the stock, ½ cup or so at a time, stirring after each addition and every minute or so. When the stock is just about evaporated, add more. The mixture should be neither soupy nor dry. Keep the heat medium to medium-high, and stir frequently.

4 Begin tasting the rice 20 minutes after you add it; you want it to be tender but with still a tiny bit of crunch. It could take as long as 30 minutes to reach this stage. When it does, add the peas, followed 1 minute later by the softened butter and Parmesan. Check the seasoning, adjust if necessary, and serve immediately.

Cooking Tips: Liquid must be added a bit at a time, and the heat must be kept fairly high. You must pay attention while making risotto. It doesn't require constant stirring, as some would have you believe, but neither should you leave the stove for more than a minute or so once you start the process.

Do not overcook. As with pasta, you should stop the cooking when there is still a tiny bit of crunch in the center of the rice kernels.

Risotto with Meat Use olive oil instead of butter. In Step 2, add 2 to 4 ounces of any of the following: ground meat (beef, pork, veal, or poultry); sausage, removed from its casing; prosciutto, country ham, or pancetta, cut into bits. You may substitute the meat for the vegetables, or add it along with them. Cook 3 to 5 minutes, stirring and breaking up any lumps that form. Proceed with the recipe, omitting the finishing butter (the Parmesan is still nice).

4 | Fish

Crisp Red Snapper or Other Fillets with Butter-Toasted Pecans

Because this recipe requires a bit of handling, and because longer cooking time means a crisper coating, it is best with sturdier fillets, such as of red snapper, catfish, sea bass, or rockfish. The technique will work with delicate fillets, but they may fall apart during cooking, and their extreme thinness means you must work in batches. Like most recipes using fish fillets, this one can be made quickly.

Makes 4 servings

Time: 30 minutes or less

1/2 cup flour

1/4 teaspoon cayenne, or to taste

1/4 teaspoon dried thyme

1 tablespoon paprika

Salt to taste

1/4 cup peanut or vegetable oil

1/2 cup milk

4 red snapper or other fillets, about 6 ounces each, scaled or skinned

4 tablespoons (1/2 stick) butter

2/3 cup pecan pieces, plus some more for garnish

Freshly ground black pepper to taste

2 tablespoons freshly squeezed lemon juice

2 tablespoons minced fresh parsley leaves

1 Mix together the flour, half the cayenne, and the thyme, paprika, and salt in a bowl. Heat the oil in a large skillet, preferably non-stick, over medium-high heat until it is good and hot (a pinch of flour will sizzle).

2 Put the milk in a bowl. Dip the fillets, one by one, in the milk; dredge them in the seasoned flour, then put them in the pan. Cook over high heat, turning once, until nicely browned on both sides; total cooking time for fillets 1/2 to 3/4 inch thick will be 5 to 6 minutes. (The fillets will be white, opaque, and tender when done.)

3 Remove the fish to a platter and keep warm; wipe out the pan and immediately melt the butter in it over medium heat. Add the pecans, the remaining cayenne, salt, and pepper, and cook, stirring frequently, until the pecans are lightly browned and fragrant, 3 to 5 minutes.

4 Add the lemon juice and parsley. Spoon a portion of nuts over each fillet and serve immediately.

Cooking Tips: With thicker fillets, those up to 1 inch or so, you can roughly estimate doneness by timing: About 8 minutes is the longest you want to cook any fillet under 1 inch thick. In addition, take a peek between the flakes of the fish; if most of the translucence is gone and the fish is tender, it's done.

Remember, all food continues to cook between stove or oven and table, and fish is so delicate that fish that is fully cooked in the kitchen will likely be slightly overcooked in the dining room.

This is one of my favorite recipes for cod and other thick fillets, because of its simplicity. Try it with red snapper, orange roughy, tilefish, or turbot, too. Increase the cooking time slightly if you use one of the sturdier fillets, such as grouper, monkfish, or striped bass. This takes some time to prepare, but you can accomplish other tasks while it is in the oven.

Makes 4 servings

Time: 1 hour

6 tablespoons (¾ stick) butter

2 to 3 pounds waxy red or white potatoes

Salt and freshly ground black pepper to taste

1 or 2 cod fillets, or other thick fillets, about 1½ pounds

1 Preheat the oven to 425°F. Place 4 tablespoons butter in a large baking dish. Put the dish in the oven while it preheats to melt the butter.

2 Peel the potatoes and slice them about ⅛ to ¼ inch thick. (I use a food processor or a mandoline for this.) Remove the pan from the oven when the butter is melted. When the oven is hot, stir the potatoes into the butter and sprinkle them liberally with salt and pepper. Return the dish to the oven and set a timer for 10 minutes.

3 Every 10 minutes, turn the potatoes gently with a spatula. When they are browned all over—30 to 40 minutes—place the cod on top of them, dotting the fish with the remaining butter. Roast the cod for 8 to 12 minutes, depending upon the thickness of the fillets (cod is done when it is opaque throughout and offers no resistance to a thin-bladed knife. Serve.

Shopping Tip: Note that some thick fillets—striped bass, for example, or grouper—are large enough so that you can ask for a "center cut" of the fillet. Such a fillet will be of fairly even thickness from one end to the other, minimizing the differences in doneness between portions of the fish. A portion of a cod fillet can also be cut to more or less uniform thickness.

Cooking Tip: Begin checking the fish after about 7 minutes of cooking time per inch of thickness. First, insert a very thin-bladed knife or skewer into the thickest part. If it penetrates with little or no resistance, the fish is done, or nearly so.

ⓦ Roast Cod or Other Thick White Fillet with Potatoes, Onions, and Olive Oil
In Step 1, gently heat 4 tablespoons of olive oil instead of butter. In Step 2, add 2 cups of sliced onions to the potatoes. In Step 3, drizzle the cod with 1 tablespoon additional olive oil. Finish as above.

Skewers of Swordfish, Tuna, or Other Steaks

Skewered fish is becoming more popular, and rightfully so: It's flavorful, fast-cooking, and always tender.

Makes 4 to 6 servings

Time: 1 hour, plus time to preheat the grill

---

1 to 1½ pounds swordfish, tuna, or other steaks (see Tips, below right), cut into 1- to 1½-inch chunks

3 medium onions, quartered

6 medium-to-large button or 2 portobello mushrooms, trimmed and quartered

6 bay leaves

6 slices bacon, cut into 3 or 4 pieces each (optional)

Salt and freshly ground black pepper to taste

1 teaspoon dried thyme, marjoram, oregano, mint, or fennel seeds

¼ cup olive oil

Juice of 1 lemon

1 Thread the swordfish onto 6 skewers, alternating with pieces of onion, mushroom, bay leaf, and bacon. Lay the skewers on a platter and sprinkle with salt, pepper, and herb. Drizzle with the oil and lemon juice and let sit for about 30 minutes, turning occasionally.

2 Start a charcoal or wood fire or preheat a gas grill or broiler; the heat should be high, but the rack 6 inches or more from the heat source.

3 Grill the skewers for 12 minutes or a little more, turning occasionally. When they're done, the bacon should be cooked but not crisp, the swordfish browned but still moist (try a piece).

Shopping Tip: Try some of these boneless fish steaks, instead of the swordfish: bluefish (delicate but strong-flavored); mako; monkfish (not a true steak, but works well in steak recipes).

Cooking Tips: Because they are of uniform thickness, or nearly so, steaks cook evenly. The problem is that some steaks—most notably swordfish and tuna—are better when they're cooked to a medium, and even a medium-rare, stage. Others, such as halibut and cod, become quite dry if they're overcooked.

Swordfish is at its most moist if you stop cooking when just a little translucence remains in the center; cook it to the well-done stage if you prefer, but get it off the heat quickly or it will be dry. Tuna is best when still red to pink in the center. Fully cooked tuna is inevitably dry.

Skewers of Swordfish, Tuna, or Other Steaks with Rosemary If you have a large rosemary bush, use long branches to skewer swordfish chunks before grilling, brushing with olive oil and lemon. If not, follow this recipe: Thread swordfish onto skewers as in Step 1, with or without vegetables. Make a marinade of 1 small onion, minced; the minced zest and juice of 1 lemon; ⅓ cup olive oil; salt and pepper; and 1 tablespoon minced fresh rosemary or 1 teaspoon dried rosemary. Step 2 remains the same. In Step 3, toss a handful of fresh rosemary or a few rosemary branches directly onto the coals before grilling. Proceed as above.

Crispy-Skin Salmon with Gingery Greens

One of my all-time favorites, this features the rich flavor of salmon cut by sharp greens sparked with ginger. Steam the greens in advance if it's more convenient for you.

Makes 4 servings

Time: 40 minutes to 1 hour, plus time to preheat the grill

---

1 (2-pound) salmon fillet, skin on (but scaled), pin bones removed

1 pound kale, collards, or other greens

About 5 tablespoons olive oil

1 teaspoon minced garlic

2 teaspoons peeled and minced or grated fresh ginger or 1 teaspoon ground ginger

1 tablespoon soy sauce

1 teaspoon dark sesame oil

1　Rinse the fish well and let it rest between paper towels, refrigerated, while you prepare the greens.

2　Wash the greens in several changes of water, and remove any pieces of stem thicker than 1/4 inch in diameter. Steam or boil them in a medium covered saucepan over 1 inch of water until good and soft, 10 minutes or more, depending on the green (older collards will require 30 minutes). Drain them, rinse in cool water, squeeze dry, and chop.

3　Preheat a covered gas grill or start a charcoal fire in a grill that can be covered. Heat 2 tablespoons of the olive oil in a large non-stick sauté pan. Add the garlic and cook 1 minute; do not brown. Add the greens and cook, stirring occasionally, for about 3 minutes; add the ginger and cook another minute, then add the soy sauce and sesame oil and turn off the heat. Remove to a platter and keep warm.

4　With a sharp knife, score the skin of the salmon in a cross-hatch pattern. Oil the fish well with the remaining olive oil. Put the fillet on the preheated grill, skin side down, and cover; alternatively, broil the salmon 4 inches from the heat source, skin side up. In either case, cook undisturbed for 5 to 10 minutes, or until done.

5　Remove the fish carefully with a large spatula, and place it on top of the greens. Serve immediately, making sure everyone gets a piece of skin.

Preparation Tip: Most fillets of salmon sold in supermarkets are NOT scaled. Usually that's not a problem; you can remove the skin after cooking. But here, the skin is an asset, so you may have to scale the fish yourself. Fortunately, though it's slightly messy, it's easy: Put the fish in the sink and, using an ordinary tablespoon, scrape the skin from the tail toward the head. See the scales come flying off? Keep going until they're all gone, then rinse.

ⓦ Sautéed Trout

There are countless ways to pan-fry trout, from the simple to the complex. If you catch your own fish, the simpler you cook it, the better.

Makes 2 servings

Time: 30 minutes

---

2 whole trout, about ¾ pound each, gutted and split or filleted

4 tablespoons (½ stick) butter or olive oil

1 cup cornmeal

Salt and freshly ground black pepper to taste

Minced fresh parsley leaves for garnish

1 Rinse and dry the fish. Melt the butter over medium-high heat in a large non-stick skillet. When the foam subsides, dredge the fish in the cornmeal, place in the pan, and raise the heat to high.

2 Season with salt and pepper and cook on both sides until nicely browned and the interior turns white, 8 to 12 minutes total. Garnish and serve.

ⓦ **Sautéed Trout with Bacon** In Step 1, omit the butter. Cook 4 slices of good bacon in a skillet. When the bacon is nice and crisp, remove it to a warm oven. Proceed as above, cooking the cornmeal-coated trout in the bacon fat. Garnish with the bacon slices and parsley.

ⓦ **Sautéed Trout with Almonds (Trout Amandine)** In Step 1, melt 1 tablespoon of butter in a small skillet over medium heat; when the foam subsides, cook ½ cup blanched slivered almonds, stirring frequently, until they start to brown, 2 or 3 minutes. Remove from the heat. Melt 3 tablespoons butter as in Step 1 and continue with the recipe. When the fish is done, garnish with the cooked almonds and the parsley, drizzle with a little freshly squeezed lemon juice, and serve.

Roast Shrimp with Tomatoes

If you have nice, juicy tomatoes to moisten the bread crumbs, stick to these proportions. If your tomatoes are dry, cut back on the bread crumbs or increase the butter a little.

Makes 4 servings

Time: 30 minutes

---

4 tablespoons (½ stick) butter, more or less, or use extra-virgin olive oil

¾ cup plain bread crumbs, preferably fresh

½ cup minced fresh parsley leaves

1 teaspoon minced garlic

Salt and freshly ground black pepper to taste

1½ to 2 pounds shrimp, in the 20 to 30 per pound range, peeled, rinsed, and dried

About 12 thick slices ripe tomato

1 Preheat the oven to 450°F. Melt about half the butter over medium heat in a large non-stick skillet, then toss in the bread crumbs, parsley, and garlic. Cook until the bread crumbs are nicely browned, stirring occasionally, and the mixture is fragrant. Turn off the heat and let it cool a bit, then season with salt and pepper.

2 Spread 1 teaspoon or so of the remaining butter around the bottom of a 9 × 13-inch baking dish, then arrange the shrimp in the dish; sprinkle with salt and pepper. Cover with about half the bread crumb mixture, then arrange the tomatoes on top. Sprinkle with the remaining bread crumbs and dot with the remaining butter. Bake until the shrimp are pink and hot, 8 to 12 minutes, depending on the size of the shrimp.

W Curried Shrimp

This is a good dish for a party, because you can make the sauce hours in advance, then add the shrimp and lemon juice at the last minute.

Makes 4 to 6 servings

Time: 45 minutes

---

2 tablespoons peanut or vegetable oil

2 large onions, minced

1 tablespoon curry powder

¼ teaspoon cayenne, or to taste

2 tablespoons minced cilantro leaves

1 pound small waxy red or white potatoes, peeled and halved

2 cups cored and chopped canned or fresh tomatoes, with their liquid

Salt to taste

1 to 1½ pounds shrimp, in the 20 to 30 per pound range, peeled, rinsed, dried, and cut into halves or thirds

2 tablespoons freshly squeezed lemon juice

1 Heat the oil over medium heat in a large skillet for 2 minutes. Add the onions and cook, stirring, until golden, about 10 minutes.

2 Add the curry powder, cayenne, and half the cilantro and stir. Add the potatoes, tomatoes, and salt; stir, cover, and cook over low heat, stirring occasionally, until the potatoes are tender, about 30 minutes.

3 Add the shrimp and lemon juice and cook, uncovered, until the shrimp turn pink, 3 to 5 minutes. Add the remaining cilantro and serve with white rice.

Grilled Scallops with Basil Stuffing

This is among the most impressive and wonderful dishes I know; the hardest part is finding good sea scallops and fresh basil. Feel free to make it on the stove top if you don't want to grill: Just heat a large, deep skillet and brown the scallops on both sides, with only the oil that clings to them.

Makes 4 servings

Time: 30 minutes, plus time to preheat the grill

1/2 cup fresh basil leaves

1 clove garlic, peeled

1 teaspoon salt

1/4 teaspoon freshly ground black pepper

1/3 cup plus 1 tablespoon extra-virgin olive oil

1 1/2 pounds or more large sea scallops

Lemon wedges

1 Mince the basil, garlic, salt, and pepper together until very fine, almost a puree (you can do this in a food processor, but it really won't save you time or effort). Mix in a small bowl or cup with 1 tablespoon of the olive oil.

2 Make a deep horizontal slit in the side of each of the scallops, but don't cut all the way through. Fill each scallop with about 1/2 teaspoon of the basil mixture; close. Pour the remaining oil onto a plate or pan and turn the scallops in it. Let sit while you preheat a gas grill or start a charcoal fire; it should be very hot before grilling, with the rack about 4 inches from the heat source.

3 Place the scallops on the grill (don't pour the remaining oil over them, as it will catch fire), and grill 2 to 3 minutes per side, no more. Serve immediately, with lemon wedges.

Shopping Tips: The best scallops, depending on your wealth and geographic orientation, are either genuine bay scallops from Nantucket, Cape Cod, or Long Island, or sea scallops. (I'm going to ignore pink scallops, which are almost never seen outside of the Northwest and are not even common there.) The least desirable (and of course the least expensive), are the tiny calicos, not much bigger than pencil erasers and just as rubbery when overcooked.

Many scallops are soaked in phosphates, which cause them to absorb water and lose flavor. Always buy scallops from someone you trust, and let him or her know that you want unsoaked (sometimes called "dry") scallops.

Preparation Tip: Note that all scallops are sold with their tendon, a stark-white strip of gristle that attaches the muscle to the shell. It is often overlooked, and can be, especially with smaller scallops. But if you are cooking just a few scallops, or have a little extra time, just strip it off with your fingers. This is an added refinement, far from essential but worthwhile.

Steamed Mussels

When mussels are good—fat and sweet—1 pound per person is just about right for a main course. A little bit of saffron added to the steaming liquid gives the broth a wondrous flavor. Serve with crusty bread to soak up the extra broth.

Makes 4 servings

Time: About 15 minutes, plus cleaning time

3 tablespoons extra-virgin olive oil

4 cloves garlic, smashed

1 medium onion, roughly sliced

½ cup dry white wine

½ cup roughly chopped fresh parsley leaves

At least 4 pounds large mussels, well washed

1 In a large pot over medium heat, heat the oil, then add the garlic and onion and cook, stirring, just until the onion softens.

2 Add the wine, parsley, and mussels, cover the pot, and turn the heat to high. Steam, shaking the pot frequently, until the mussels open, about 8 to 10 minutes. Use a slotted spoon to put the mussels into a serving bowl; if you like, you can strain a little of the liquid over them.

Preparation Tip: Farmed mussels are almost always cleaner than wild mussels and will require no more than a quick rinse and removal of the "beard," the weedy growth attached to the bottom of the shell. Wild mussels (which usually taste better) require washing in several changes of water. Discard any mussels with broken shells, those whose shells remain open after tapping them lightly, or those which seem unusually heavy—chances are they're filled with mud. As long as you do this, any mussels that don't open fully during cooking are still safe to eat; just pry apart their shells with a knife.

Mussels with Butter Sauce Follow the basic recipe and keep the mussels warm. Strain the cooking liquid through a sieve lined with a paper towel into a medium saucepan and bring it to a boil over medium-high heat. Meanwhile, discard 1 shell of each mussel, and arrange the remaining shells, with the mussel meat, on a platter. Keep warm in a low oven while the liquid reduces. When the steaming liquid is reduced to about ¼ cup, add 3 tablespoons butter, cut into bits, and let it melt. Add 1 teaspoon minced garlic and ¼ cup minced fresh parsley leaves. Cook over medium heat for a minute or two. Check for salt, then drizzle the sauce over the mussel meats and serve.

Debearding Mussels

Most mussels have a "beard," a small amount of vegetative growth extending from their flat side. Pull or cut it off before cooking.

Sautéed Soft-Shell Crabs

Spring brings one of the best treats of all to fish counters: soft-shell crabs. They are a strange delight (everyone gets at least a little squeamish when first biting into a whole crab), but are nothing more than the familiar blue crabs caught just after they have molted, or shed, their hard outer shell.

Makes 2 to 4 servings

Time: 20 minutes (with cleaned soft-shells)

---

4 tablespoons (½ stick) butter, olive oil, or a combination, plus more if needed

4 soft-shell crabs, cleaned and dried thoroughly

Flour for dredging

1 egg lightly beaten with 1 tablespoon water

Plain bread crumbs for dredging, seasoned with salt and freshly ground black pepper

Lemon wedges or Vinaigrette (page 19)

1 Heat a large non-stick skillet over medium-high heat for 2 or 3 minutes.

2 Melt the butter in the skillet and, when the foam subsides, dredge a crab in flour, dip it in the egg, then dredge it in the bread crumbs, and place it in the skillet. Repeat the process (depending upon the size of your crabs, you may have to cook in two batches; add more fat if necessary).

3 Cook the crabs—covering the skillet if you like—until golden brown on one side, then turn and cook until golden brown on the other, about 4 minutes per side. Serve immediately, with lemon wedges.

Shopping Tip: Estimate 2 soft-shell crabs per serving for average appetites, although eating 3 or 4 is not that difficult.

Preparation Tip: Have your fishmonger clean the live soft crabs, then when you get them home, you can: eat them, refrigerate them (for a day or two only), or freeze them.

Cooking Tip: Soft-shells spatter when fried; if you don't want to mess up the kitchen, cover them for the first 2 minutes of cooking. They will not be as crisp, but they will still be delicious and you won't regret cooking them during the 20 minutes it will take you to clean up after the meal.

5 | Poultry

Roast Chicken with Rice-and-Nut Stuffing

Roast chicken is the ultimate in simple elegance, but there are times you'll want to stuff a chicken for various reasons: to make it seem more festive, because the bird is big enough to carve, or just because you feel like it.

Makes 4 to 6 servings

Time: 1½ hours

½ cup long-grain white rice (basmati is best)

4 tablespoons olive oil or butter

¼ cup pine nuts or shelled pistachio nuts

2 tablespoons raisins or currants (optional)

Salt and freshly ground black pepper to taste

2 tablespoons freshly squeezed lemon juice

1 tablespoon minced fresh marjoram or oregano leaves or 1 teaspoon dried

1 whole 4½- to 6-pound chicken, trimmed of excess fat, interior cavity carefully cleaned, rinsed and patted dry with paper towels

1 Bring a large pot of water to boil; salt it. Add the rice and simmer, stirring occasionally, until it is tender but not at all mushy, 8 to 10 minutes. Drain it, rinse it, and drain it again. Preheat the oven to 400°F.

2 Heat 2 tablespoons of the oil or butter in a large, deep skillet over medium heat for 2 minutes. Toss in the nuts and the raisins or currants, if you are using them, and stir for 1 minute. Add the rice and stir, seasoning with salt and pepper, while cooking for another minute; the rice need not get hot. Add the lemon juice and half the herb. (You may prepare the recipe in advance up to this point; refrigerate, well wrapped or in a covered container, for up to 2 days before proceeding.)

3 Stuff the chicken loosely with this mixture. Do not overstuff; if there's extra stuffing, just heat some up later and serve it on the side. Truss the chicken if you like (see illustrations, at right; this will help keep the stuffing in the bird). Rub the chicken with 1 tablespoon of the remaining olive oil or butter and season it with salt and pepper. Place it on a rack in a roasting pan, breast side up, and put the pan in the oven.

4 Roast the chicken for at least 1¼ hours (depending on its size; a larger bird will take longer), basting with the remaining tablespoon of oil or butter about halfway through, and any pan juices that accumulate. The bird is done when an instant-read thermometer inserted into the thickest part of the thigh reads 160° to 165°F.

5 Remove chicken from oven and let rest for 5 minutes. Carve, garnish with reserved herb, and serve with stuffing and pan juices.

Shopping Tip: Years ago, chickens were labeled fryers, broilers, pullets, hens, and fowl, according to size, sex, and age. Now, you rarely see anything other than frying/broiling chickens (anything under 4 pounds or so) and roasting chickens (anything larger). "Fowl," also labeled "stewing chicken," is a large bird that is likely to be tough unless cooked in liquid; it should be quite flavorful in a dish such as Chicken in a Pot (page 64). But most commercial fowl is best used for stock.

Roast Stuffed Chicken with Roast Vegetables If you're using a larger bird—5 or 6 pounds—you can roast vegetables using the same heat and cooking times as above. (At this relatively low temperature, vegetables will not become tender with a smaller bird, which will be cooked in 1¼ hours.) Use about 2 pounds of any root or other winter vegetables—carrots, celery, white or sweet potatoes, winter squash, garlic, and so on. Peel the vegetables and make sure that no piece is greater than 1½ inches in diameter, preferably smaller. When you remove the chicken in Step 5, if the vegetables are not quite done, raise the heat to 450°F and roast while you rest and carve the chicken; it won't be long.

Roast Stuffed Chicken with Pan Gravy This is best when the chicken is cooked with butter. Steps 1 through 4 remain the same. In Step 5, while the bird is resting, place the roasting pan on a burner over high heat. Add 1 cup chicken or other stock and cook, stirring and scraping the bottom of the pan to loosen any solids that have stuck there, until the liquid is reduced by about 50 percent. Turn the heat to low. Add about 1 teaspoon of the minced fresh herb you have been using along with 1 tablespoon of butter; stir until the butter melts. Serve with the chicken.

Trussing Chicken

| 1 | 2 | 3 | 4 |

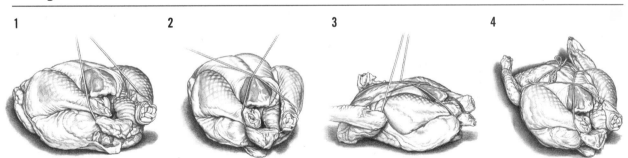

(Step 1) Use a piece of string about 3 feet long. Place the center of the string under the rear end of the bird and loop it around the ends of the legs. **(Step 2)** Cross the string over the top of the bird's breast. **(Step 3)** Loop the string under and around the wings. **(Step 4)** Tie a knot or a bow on top of the bird to join the ends of the string. Trim as necessary.

Chicken, Provençal-Style

This is a delicious stove-top chicken dish. You can add eggplant and/or zucchini to this vegetable mixture if you like, or use boneless chicken meat. Feel free, too, to substitute another herb, or a combination of herbs, for the thyme. Remove the chicken skin if you choose to skip the browning. Serve with the rice or crusty bread.

Makes 4 servings

Time: About 40 minutes

2 tablespoons olive oil

About 1 cup all-purpose flour for dredging

Salt and freshly ground black pepper to taste

1 (3- to 4-pound) chicken, cut up, with each leg cut into 2 pieces (cut through the joint where the drumstick meets the thigh), trimmed of excess fat, then rinsed and patted dry with paper towels

2 medium onions, chopped

2 anchovy fillets, minced (optional)

1 teaspoon minced garlic

2 cups cored and chopped tomatoes (canned are fine; don't bother to drain)

1/4 teaspoon cayenne (optional)

1/2 cup dry white wine, Full-Flavored Chicken Stock (page 20), store-bought chicken or vegetable broth, or water

1 cup Niçoise or other good black olives

1/2 teaspoon fresh thyme leaves or 1/4 teaspoon dried thyme

Minced fresh parsley leaves for garnish

1 Heat the oil over medium-high heat in a large, deep skillet. Put the flour on a plate or in a shallow bowl and season it with salt and pepper. When the oil is hot (a pinch of flour will sizzle), dredge the chicken pieces in the flour (thighs first, followed by drumsticks, then finally breasts and wings), shaking off any excess. As you coat the chicken pieces, add them to the oil and brown on all sides. Regulate the heat so that the oil bubbles but is not so hot that it will burn the chicken. Season the pieces with salt and pepper as they brown. (You can skip this browning step if you like, as noted above; heat the oil and go directly to cooking the onions.)

2 When the chicken is nicely browned, remove it from the skillet and turn the heat to medium. Pour or spoon off all but a tablespoon of the oil. Add the onions and anchovies; cook over medium heat until the onions soften, about 5 minutes. Add the garlic, tomatoes, and cayenne, if desired, and raise the heat slightly. Cook until some of the tomato juice bubbles away, 1 to 2 minutes. Add the wine or other liquid and cook another 2 minutes.

3 Add the olives and the thyme, along with some salt (remember that the olives are salty) and pepper. Cook 1 minute; submerge the chicken in the sauce, cover, and cook over medium-low heat, turning the pieces every 5 minutes or so, until the chicken is cooked through, 20 to 30 minutes (longer if you skipped the browning step). Garnish and serve immediately.

Cooking Tip: In any chicken recipe, care must be taken when cooking white and dark meat together, since white meat cooks so much faster. Sometimes, the thickness of a bone-in breast compensates for the difference, and everything finishes at about the same time. You can also increase the likelihood of even cooking by starting the legs a little before the breasts and by keeping them in the hottest part of the pan (usually the center, if you're cooking on top of the stove).

ⓦ Chicken with Onions A simpler version of the recipe at left. In Step 2, double the amount of onions and omit anchovies, garlic, tomatoes, and cayenne. Include the wine as above. In Step 3, omit the olives but use the thyme. Proceed as outlined.

ⓦ Chicken with Rice (Arroz con Pollo) In Step 2, cook the onions without anchovies as above; when they're soft, add 1 tablespoon minced garlic and 2 cups long-grain white rice; cook, stirring, until the rice is coated with oil. Omit tomatoes, cayenne, wine, olives, and thyme. Return the chicken to the pan with some salt and pepper. With the heat on medium, add 4 cups liquid—chicken, meat, or vegetable broth, or water, or a combination—and stir gently. Cover the pan, reduce the heat to medium-low, and cook, lowering the heat as necessary to maintain a very gentle simmer. Cook until all the water is absorbed and the chicken is cooked through, about 30 minutes. Adjust the seasonings as necessary, garnish, and serve.

Dried porcini, red wine, and tomatoes make this rich, classic, dark-sauced dish, akin to the famous *coq au vin*.

Makes 4 servings

Time: About 40 minutes

1 ounce dried porcini mushrooms

2 tablespoons olive oil

About 1 cup all-purpose flour for dredging

Salt and freshly ground black pepper to taste

1 whole (3- to 4-pound) chicken, cut up, with each leg cut into 2 pieces (cut through the joint where the drumstick meets the thigh), trimmed of excess fat, then rinsed and patted dry with paper towels

2 tablespoons butter, or more olive oil

½ pound white button mushrooms, trimmed and sliced

2 medium onions, chopped

1 teaspoon minced garlic

Salt and freshly ground black pepper to taste

1 sprig fresh thyme or ½ teaspoon dried thyme

1 bay leaf

1 cup dry red wine

¼ cup minced fresh parsley leaves, plus more for garnish

1 Soak dried porcini mushrooms in hot water to cover while you proceed with the recipe.

2 Heat the oil over medium-high heat in a large, deep skillet, Dutch oven, or casserole. Put the flour on a plate or in a shallow bowl and season it with salt and pepper. When the oil is hot (a pinch of flour will sizzle), dredge the chicken pieces in the flour (thighs first, followed by drumsticks, then finally breasts and wings), shaking off any excess. As you coat the pieces, add them to the oil and brown on all sides. Regulate the heat so that the oil bubbles but is not so hot that it will burn the chicken. (You can skip this browning step if you like, as noted above; heat the oil and go directly to cooking the mushrooms.)

3 When the chicken is nicely browned, remove it from the skillet and turn the heat to medium. Pour off all the fat and add the butter or additional oil. A minute later, add the white mushrooms.

4 Cook, stirring, until the mushrooms begin to darken, about 5 minutes. Drain the porcini and reserve their liquid. Chop the porcini mushrooms and add them and a little of their liquid (pour carefully, or strain it first if it is gritty), along with the onions, garlic, salt, pepper, and thyme. Cook until the onions soften, about 5 minutes.

5 Add the bay leaf, wine, parsley, the remaining mushroom soaking liquid, and the chicken. Cover, turn the heat to low, and cook, turning the pieces every 5 minutes or so, until the chicken is cooked through, 20 to 30 minutes (longer if you skipped the browning step). Remove the cover. If the sauce is too watery, raise the heat to high and cook, stirring and scraping the bottom of the pan, until the liquid is reduced slightly. Adjust the seasoning if necessary, then garnish and serve.

Preparation Tip: It pays to cut chicken legs in two, to help them cook more quickly. In any case, keep an eye on things and remove the breasts as soon as they're done, even if the legs have a few minutes more to go. When measured with an instant-read thermometer, breasts are done at 160°F, thighs closer to 165°F.

Chicken Adobo

This Philippine classic has been called the best chicken dish in the world by a number of friends of mine. The chicken is cooked in liquid first, then roasted. The initial poaching sauce is reduced to become a sauce to pass at the table for both the chicken and white rice, the natural accompaniment to this dish.

You can make Chicken Adobo in two steps, first poaching and then broiling or grilling, refrigerating the chicken and the sauce in between. If you do this, skim the fat from the sauce before reheating.

Makes 4 servings

Time: About 1¼ hours, plus time to preheat the grill

---

1 cup soy sauce

½ cup white or rice vinegar

1 cup water

1 tablespoon chopped garlic

2 bay leaves

½ teaspoon freshly ground black pepper

1 whole (3- to 4-pound) chicken, cut up (legs cut in two), trimmed of excess fat, then rinsed and patted dry with paper towels; or use 2 pounds bone-in thighs

1 Combine the first six ingredients in a covered pot large enough to hold the chicken in one layer. Bring to a boil over high heat. Add the chicken; reduce the heat to medium-low and cook, covered, for about 30 minutes, turning once or twice. (You may prepare the recipe in advance up to this point; refrigerate the chicken, in the liquid, for up to a day before proceeding.)

2 Start a charcoal or wood fire or preheat a gas grill or broiler. The fire need not be too hot, but place the rack just 3 or 4 inches from the heat source.

3 Remove the chicken and dry it gently with paper towels. Boil the sauce over high heat until it is reduced to about 1 cup; discard the bay leaves and keep the sauce warm. Meanwhile, grill or broil the chicken until brown and crisp, about 5 minutes per side. Serve the chicken with the sauce and white rice.

Chicken in a Pot

The original one-pot dinner. Serve it one of two ways: as a stew with everything in the bowl; or as a plain broth (garnish with dill or parsley), followed by the chicken and vegetables on a platter.

Canned broth serves very nicely here, since its flavor is increased by the chicken and vegetables during the simmering time. If you don't have any stock or broth at all, remove the chicken's backbone and wing tips and simmer them along with the neck and gizzard in 8 cups water for about 30 minutes before starting; fish them out before adding the other ingredients.

Makes 4 servings

Time: About 1½ hours

1 whole (3- to 4-pound) chicken, trimmed of excess fat, then rinsed and patted dry with paper towels

8 cups Full-Flavored Chicken Stock (page 20, see headnote) or chicken broth

3 onions, quartered

2 large or 4 small-to-medium carrots, peeled and cut into chunks

2 leeks, split, trimmed, cleaned, and cut into 2-inch lengths

1 bay leaf

4 allspice berries

10 whole peppercorns

4 sprigs fresh thyme or 1 teaspoon dried thyme

Salt and freshly ground black pepper to taste

Minced fresh parsley or dill leaves for garnish

1 Put the chicken in a large pot with the stock, onions, carrots, and leeks. Bring to a boil over medium-high heat, then immediately reduce heat to medium-low. Skim foam from the surface if necessary.

2 Add the bay leaf, allspice, peppercorns, and thyme to the pot along with some salt and pepper. Simmer about 45 minutes, until the chicken and vegetables are nearly tender and the chicken is cooked through. With 15 minutes of cooking time remaining, preheat the oven to 200°F.

3 When the chicken is done, use a slotted spoon to remove it and the vegetables to an ovenproof platter and place the platter in the oven.

4 Raise the heat to high and boil the stock until it reduces by about 25 percent, 10 to 15 minutes.

5 Strain the stock into a large bowl or another large pot and adjust the seasoning as needed. Serve the soup as a first course, garnished with parsley or dill, followed by the chicken and vegetables, or cut up the chicken (see page 67) and serve in deep bowls with the broth and the vegetables. Garnish each serving with parsley or dill.

Preparation Tip: Leeks must be washed thoroughly before using; they contain a great deal of sand. Split them in half lengthwise (they're a little easier to handle if you leave them attached at the root end for now), then rinse carefully, fanning out the layers to make sure you get every last trace of sand. Then cut off the root and chop the leeks as necessary.

Chili-Spiced Fried Chicken

Like all good fried-chicken dishes, this one is fine at room temperature—great for picnics and buffets. If you want simpler chicken, omit the chili powder, cumin, turmeric, and cayenne; serve with lemon wedges.

Makes 4 to 6 servings

Time: About 30 minutes

Peanut oil, vegetable oil, or a combination for frying

2 cups all-purpose flour

2 tablespoons chili powder

2 tablespoons ground cumin

2 teaspoons ground turmeric

1/2 teaspoon cayenne (optional)

1 tablespoon coarse salt

1 teaspoon freshly ground black pepper

1 whole (3- to 4-pound) chicken, cut up, trimmed of excess fat, then rinsed and patted dry with paper towels

Lime wedges (optional)

1 Heat about 1/2 inch of the fat over medium-high heat in a deep-fryer, large, deep skillet, or broad saucepan that can later be covered. While it is heating, mix together the flour and seasonings in a plastic bag. Toss the chicken in the bag, 2 or 3 pieces at a time, until they are well coated with flour. Put them on a rack as you finish.

2 When the fat reaches 350°F, raise the heat to high and begin to slowly but steadily add the chicken pieces, skin side down, to the skillet (if you add them all at once, the temperature will plummet). When they have all been added, cover the skillet, reduce the heat to medium-high, and set a timer for 7 minutes. After 7 minutes, uncover the skillet, turn the chicken, and continue to cook, uncovered, for another 7 minutes.

3 Turn the chicken skin side down again and cook for about 5 minutes more, turning as necessary to ensure that both sides are golden brown.

4 As the chicken pieces finish cooking (the juices near the bone will run clear), remove them from the skillet and drain them on paper towels. Serve hot, warm, or at room temperature with lime wedges, if desired.

Shopping Tip: Peanut oil works well for frying. If cost is an issue, use the least expensive vegetable oil you can find, such as soy or canola; as long as the oil is clean, its flavor will be neutral.

Cooking Tips: To reduce the messiness of spattering frying oil, I use a minimum of oil (which still seems like a lot by today's standards), and I cover the skillet for the first few minutes, which reduces spattering substantially. Then I uncover the chicken to make sure it doesn't steam in its own juices, which would defeat the point of frying—namely, a super-crisp skin and moist interior.

Use a frying thermometer for frying accuracy; too-low temperatures will result in soggy chicken. As with any fried foods, the temperature will plunge as soon as you begin to add the chicken, so keep the heat as high as possible at first to enable the temperature to recover as quickly as possible. Don't crowd, either; if the chicken pieces touch each other, they won't brown at all.

Roast Duck

By itself, a duck doesn't really serve four, but it can be adequate if your co-eaters are not big on meat and you serve plenty of side dishes.

Makes 2 to 4 servings

Time: About 1¼ hours

---

1 (4- to 5-pound) duck, excess fat removed, rinsed and patted dry with paper towels

Salt and freshly ground black pepper to taste

1 tablespoon soy sauce (optional)

1 Preheat the oven to 350°F. Prick the duck skin all over with a sharp fork, skewer, or thin-bladed knife; try not to hit the meat (the fat layer is usually about ¼ inch thick). Season the duck with salt and pepper and place it, breast side down, on a rack in a roasting pan.

2 Roast the duck for 15 minutes, prick the exposed skin again, then roast another 15 minutes. Brush with a little soy sauce, if desired, and then turn it breast side up. Prick again, brush with a little more soy sauce, then roast until the meat is done, about another 45 minutes; all juices, including those from the center vent, should run clear, and the leg bone should wiggle a little in its socket. When the bird is done, an instant-read thermometer inserted into the thigh will measure about 180°F. Raise the heat to 400°F for the last 10 minutes of cooking if the duck is not as brown as you'd like.

3 Carve the duck (at right) and serve.

Shopping Tip: "Duck" usually means Peking duck, the kind found in every supermarket. It's usually sold "fresh" but in fact is shipped frozen and then thawed; truly fresh duck is rare. All duck has dark meat that is far richer than that of chicken.

Preparation Tip: To get rid of some of the fat under the duck's skin, I use the method my mother taught me: You prick the skin as the bird roasts. It's a bit of a nuisance, and sometimes makes a mess of the oven, but it works brilliantly. And, if you roast in an empty pan, you get a great deal of nice, clean fat that you can save (it keeps for weeks in the refrigerator, months in the freezer) for cooking other dishes in which you want a flavor boost.

Carving Small Roasted Birds

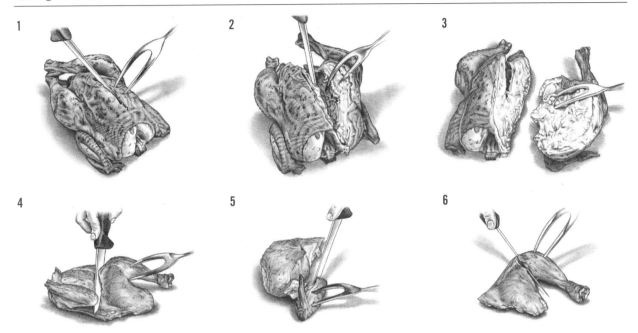

(Step 1) For chicken, duck, and other small birds, cut straight down on either side of the breastbone, following the shape of the carcass. **(Step 2)** Continue to cut down toward the back until you reach the joints holding the thigh and wing to the carcass. **(Step 3)** Cut through those joints to free the entire half of the bird. **(Step 4)** Separate leg and breast sections by cutting through the skin that holds them together; hold the knife almost parallel to the cutting board, cut from the breast toward the leg, and you will easily find the right spot. **(Step 5)** Separate the wing from the breast if you like. **(Step 6)** Separate leg and thigh; the joint will offer little resistance once you find it.

Grilled or Broiled Cornish Hens

Cornish hens are tiny, just over 1 pound each. They serve one or two people each and are great split before cooking. This light sauce works well with any grilled poultry, from chicken to squab. Good with rabbit, too.

Makes 2 to 4 servings

Time: About 40 minutes, plus time to preheat the grill

---

2 Cornish hens, about 1 pound each, rinsed and patted dry with paper towels

1 cup Full-Flavored Chicken Stock (page 20) or store-bought chicken, beef, or other broth

2 tablespoons any good vinegar

Salt and freshly ground black pepper to taste

Minced fresh parsley leaves for garnish

1 Start a wood or charcoal fire or preheat a gas grill or broiler; the fire should be moderately hot. Remove the backbone of the hens by cutting along their length on either side. Boil the stock in a small saucepan until reduced by about half; stir in the vinegar and some salt and pepper if necessary.

2 Grill or broil the hens 4 to 6 inches from the heat source, turning frequently so they brown but do not burn, and seasoning them with salt and pepper. Toward the end of their cooking time (which will be 20 to 30 minutes total, depending on the intensity of the heat), begin basting the hens with the vinegar sauce. When the hens are done, sprinkle them with the remaining sauce. Garnish and serve hot or at room temperature.

Wine-Braised Quail with Herbs

Quail is so small (you need two per serving) and lean that it inevitably dries out unless it's cooked with liquid; treated this way, it becomes succulent and delicious. It is sometimes sold fresh but is often available frozen in many supermarkets.

Makes 4 to 8 servings, depending on the number of side dishes

Time: Less than 1 hour

2 tablespoons olive oil, plus more if needed

About 1 cup all-purpose flour for dredging

8 quail, split in half (below), excess fat removed, rinsed and patted dry with paper towels

Salt and freshly ground black pepper to taste

1 cup dry white wine

2 ripe tomatoes (or use canned, drained), peeled, cored, seeded, and chopped

1 tablespoon minced fresh sage leaves or 1 teaspoon crumbled dried sage; or 1 teaspoon fresh thyme or rosemary leaves or ½ teaspoon dried thyme or rosemary

Minced fresh parsley leaves for garnish

1 Heat the oil over medium-high heat in a large, deep skillet, Dutch oven, or casserole. Put the flour on a plate or in a shallow bowl. When the oil is hot (a pinch of flour will sizzle), dredge the quail halves lightly in the flour, shaking off any excess. Add them one at a time to the oil and brown on both sides; you will have to work in batches. Regulate the heat so that the oil bubbles but is not so hot that it will burn the quail. Season the pieces with salt and pepper as they brown and add additional oil if necessary.

2 When all the quail are browned, remove them from the skillet. Turn the heat to medium and add the wine, tomatoes, and herb (except the parsley garnish); bring to a boil and let cook for a minute or two. Return the quail to the skillet, turn the heat to low, cover, and cook, turning the quail occasionally, until it is tender, 25 to 30 minutes.

3 Remove the birds to a warm platter. If the sauce is watery turn the heat to high and cook, stirring and scraping the bottom of the pan, until the liquid is reduced by about half. When it's done, pour it over the quail, garnish, and serve.

Splitting Small Birds

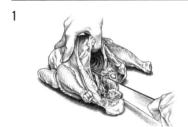
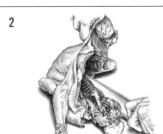

(Steps 1–2) To split chicken, quail, or other small birds: With the breast facing up, use a heavy knife to cut on either side of the backbone, cutting from front to rear. Once the backbone is removed, you will be able to lay the chicken out flat and flatten it on both sides. **(Step 3)** If you like, you can split the bird into two halves.

6 | Meat

W Grilled Marinated Flank Steak

Flank steak is best when sliced before serving, and a marinade gives each slice more flavor. You can grill the whole piece, of course, but I like to grill half of it and leave the rest in its marinade, refrigerated, for a day or two. I use some for a stir-fry and some for a salad, below. As long as you have a little time to marinate the meat, this is easy enough to make on a weeknight.

Flank steak is also good without marinating: Just coat it with curry powder, chili powder, or any other commercial or homemade spice rub before cooking.

Makes 4 to 8 servings

Time: About 1 hour, largely unattended, plus time to preheat the grill

---

4 tablespoons freshly squeezed lime juice

2 tablespoons soy sauce or fish sauce (nuoc mam or nam pla, available at Asian markets)

1 teaspoon minced garlic

1 teaspoon peeled and minced or grated fresh ginger or 1 teaspoon ground ginger

1 teaspoon sugar

Salt and freshly ground black pepper to taste

1 flank steak, 2 to 2½ pounds

1 Combine all the seasonings in a shallow bowl or platter and marinate the steak in them for at least 30 minutes (if the marinating time is longer than an hour, refrigerate). Near the end of the marinating time, start a charcoal or wood fire or preheat a gas grill or broiler; make it very hot.

2 Remove the meat from the marinade and dry well with paper towels. Grill or broil the steak about 4 inches from the heat source for 3 to 4 minutes per side, or until nicely browned. Move the meat to a cooler part of the grill (or lower the broiling rack) and cook for another 2 minutes per side. Check for doneness by touch, with a thin-bladed knife, or, preferably, with an instant-read thermometer (125°F is about right for rare to medium-rare).

3 Let rest for 5 minutes before cutting into thin slices, across the grain, using a sharp carving knife.

W Salad with Grilled Marinated Flank Steak Cut ½ recipe of flank steak, cooked as above, into chunks. Toss with 6 cups of torn washed and dried mixed lettuces (a store-bought mesclun mixture is great), and top with some quartered ripe tomatoes and sliced cucumber. Mix together 6 tablespoons freshly squeezed lime juice, 1 tablespoon soy sauce, and 2 tablespoons peanut oil; add pepper, salt if necessary, and a dash of cayenne if you like. Taste and adjust seasoning. Drizzle over the salad and serve. (Makes 4 servings.)

Roast Tenderloin with Herbs

A large piece of beef tenderloin makes a beautiful presentation.

Makes at least 10 servings

Time: At least 1½ hours, largely unattended

½ cup extra-virgin olive oil

1 tablespoon balsamic or sherry vinegar

¼ cup roughly chopped fresh parsley, stems included

1 teaspoon fresh thyme leaves, or several thyme sprigs, or ½ teaspoon dried thyme

1 bay leaf

2 cloves garlic, lightly smashed

1 (5-pound) tenderloin, trimmed of fat

Salt and freshly ground black pepper to taste

Béarnaise Sauce (at right)

1 Combine the first six ingredients; marinate the meat in this mixture for an hour or more (refrigerated if longer than an hour). When you're ready to cook, preheat the oven to 450°F.

2 Remove the meat from the marinade and pat it dry. Roast for 20 minutes, then check with meat thermometer; when the meat measures 125°F in a couple of places (since the thickness doesn't vary much, there shouldn't be much change in temperature from one spot to another) it is medium-rare; remove the roast from the oven and season with salt and pepper.

3 Let the meat rest for about 5 minutes before carving; cut into thick (at least ½ inch) slices, and serve with Béarnaise Sauce.

Béarnaise Sauce

Makes about 1 cup • Time: 20 minutes

This old-fashioned sauce has such good flavor it deserves to be made every now and then. And it is not at all difficult. You can spike béarnaise with many other seasonings: a dollop of Dijon mustard or horseradish, ½ teaspoon of finely minced raw garlic, 1 tablespoon of chopped capers, or minced fresh herbs—especially tarragon, chervil, or parsley—to taste.

1 tablespoon minced shallot	⅓ cup white wine or other vinegar
2 teaspoons minced fresh tarragon leaves or ½ teaspoon dried tarragon	2 egg yolks
	1 tablespoon water
Salt and freshly ground black pepper to taste	8 tablespoons (1 stick) butter, cut into pieces
	Freshly squeezed lemon juice, if needed

1 In a small saucepan, combine the shallot, most of the tarragon, the salt, pepper, and vinegar, and turn the heat to medium-low. Cook until all but about 2 tablespoons of the vinegar has evaporated. Cool.

2 Beat the egg yolks with the water; stir into the vinegar mixture. Return to the stove over low heat; beat continuously with a whisk until thick, about 5 minutes.

3 With the heat as low as possible, use a wooden spoon to stir in the butter a bit at a time. Add the remaining tarragon and taste; add salt and pepper if necessary and, if the taste is not quite sharp enough, a bit of lemon juice. If the sauce is too thick, stir in hot water, a teaspoon at a time. Serve immediately.

Short Ribs Simmered with Potatoes and Mustard

Most short ribs are simply the cut-off ends of the prime rib. (They may also be cut from a different part of the cow, but are treated the same.) You can grill or broil short ribs, and they are delicious; but make sure your teeth are strong and be prepared to exercise your jaw muscles.

The ideal way to cook this dish is to simmer the meat and vegetables one day, then separate them and refrigerate. The next day, you can skim the fat before finishing the dish. Or cook the whole thing in one session.

Makes 4 servings

Time: About 2 hours, or overnight, largely unattended

---

2 tablespoons any neutral vegetable or olive oil

3 pounds meaty short ribs, more or less

Salt and freshly ground black pepper to taste

2 cups minced onions

1 cup Full-Flavored Chicken Stock (page 20), store-bought chicken, beef, or vegetable broth, or water

1 pound waxy red or white potatoes, peeled, cut in half if large

Dry red wine (optional)

2 tablespoons Dijon or other good mustard

Minced fresh parsley leaves for garnish

1 Heat the oil over medium-high heat in a Dutch oven or similar pot. Brown the short ribs well on all sides, seasoning them as they cook with salt and pepper. Regulate the heat so that the ribs do not burn. This process will take 20 minutes or so; don't rush it. (You can also do the initial browning in the oven: Preheat to 500°F and roast the ribs, turning once or twice, until brown all over; time will be about the same, 20 minutes.)

2 Remove the ribs to a plate, pour off all but 2 tablespoons of the fat, and turn the heat to medium.

3 Cook the onions over medium heat until soft, stirring occasionally, about 10 minutes; stir in the stock or water, salt, and pepper. Return the ribs to the pot, bring to a boil over medium-high heat, cover, and reduce the heat to low. Cook, stirring occasionally.

4 After 30 minutes, add the potatoes. Cook, turning the ribs in the stock every 15 minutes or so, and adding a little more liquid—stock, water, or dry red wine—if the mixture seems dry. The dish is done when the meat is very tender and almost falling off the bone, and the potatoes are soft, at least another 30 minutes. (At this point you may use a slotted spoon to remove the meat and vegetables to a platter and refrigerate them and the stock overnight. The next day, skim the fat from the stock, add the meat and vegetables back to it, and reheat.) Stir the mustard into the stew, taste and adjust seasonings, garnish, and serve.

Cooking Tip: Because they're so tough, it's better to cook short ribs in liquid until they are really tender, practically mushy. Their great flavor will intensify any liquid surrounding them.

Classic Osso Buco

Osso buco literally means, "bone with hole." And it's the holes in the braised veal shank bones, which contain the creamy, delicious marrow, that make this dish so wonderful. (Yes, the meat is good too.) So when you're buying veal shank for osso buco, make sure each piece contains a nice soft center (press to check); pieces from the hind shank are meatier than those from the foreshank. The master recipe here is a rather "pure" osso buco, dominated by the flavors of veal and butter or oil. The variation is bolder, with a rich sauce that is absolutely a killer. Both are terrific.

Makes 4 servings

Time: About 2 hours, largely unattended

---

4 large veal shanks, 8 to 12 ounces each

Flour for dredging

4 tablespoons (½ stick) butter, or a combination of butter and olive oil, or all olive oil

Salt and freshly ground black pepper to taste

1 cup chopped onion

1 celery stalk, chopped

2 medium carrots, peeled and chopped

1 or 2 sprigs fresh thyme or ½ teaspoon dried thyme

¾ cup dry white wine

1 cup Full-Flavored Chicken Stock (page 20), store-bought chicken, beef, or vegetable broth, or water

1 Preheat the oven to 350°F. For a somewhat more elegant presentation, tie the shanks around their circumference with a piece of kitchen twine to prevent the meat from falling off the bone (you don't need to do this). Select a large, ovenproof casserole that can later be covered, and place it over medium-high heat for 3 to 4 minutes.

2 Dry the shanks well and dredge them in the flour. When the casserole is hot, add half the butter and/or oil. A minute later, add the shanks and brown them well on both sides, sprinkling them with salt and pepper as they cook. This will take a total of 10 to 15 minutes.

3 Remove the shanks to a plate and wipe out the casserole with a towel. Turn the heat to medium and add the remaining butter or oil. A minute later, add the vegetables and thyme. Cook, stirring occasionally, until soft, about 10 minutes, sprinkling with a little more salt and pepper. Add the wine, turn up the heat a bit, and let it bubble away for 1 minute.

4 Nestle the shanks among the vegetables and pour the stock or water over all. Cover and place in the oven. Cook for 1½ to 2 hours, turning three or four times during the cooking, or until the meat is very tender and just about falling off the bone. Remove the meat to a warm platter. If the sauce is very soupy, cook it over high heat for a few minutes to reduce it somewhat, then pour it over the meat. Serve hot, with crusty bread, and spoons or dull knives for extracting the marrow.

Osso Buco with Tomatoes, Garlic, and Anchovies Steps 1 and 2 remain unchanged. In Step 3, before adding the vegetables and thyme, cook 1 tablespoon minced garlic and 3 minced anchovy fillets in the butter and/or oil, stirring until the anchovies break up. Add the vegetables and wine as above, then add 2 cups cored and chopped tomatoes (canned are fine; drain them first). Cook until the mixture becomes saucy. Add only ½ cup of stock (the richer the better) and finish cooking as above.

Classic Beef Stew

Browning the beef before braising adds another dimension of flavor, but isn't absolutely necessary. Try it both ways; skipping the browning step saves time and mess. Note, too, that stewed beef can be spiced in many different ways; I offer a few variations here.

Makes 4 to 6 servings

Time: 1½ to 2 hours, largely unattended

---

2 tablespoons canola or other neutral oil, or olive oil

1 clove garlic, lightly crushed, plus 1 tablespoon minced garlic

2 to 2½ pounds beef chuck or round, trimmed of surface fat and cut into 1- to 1½-inch cubes

Salt and freshly ground black pepper to taste

2 large or 3 medium onions, cut into eighths

3 tablespoons flour

3 cups Full-Flavored Chicken Stock (page 20), store-bought chicken, beef, or vegetable broth, water, wine, or a combination

1 bay leaf

1 teaspoon fresh thyme leaves or ½ teaspoon dried thyme

4 medium-to-large potatoes, peeled and cut into 1-inch chunks

4 large carrots, peeled and cut into 1-inch chunks

1 cup fresh or frozen (thawed) peas

Minced fresh parsley leaves for garnish

1 Heat a large casserole or deep skillet that can later be covered over medium-high heat for 2 or 3 minutes; add the oil and the crushed garlic clove; cook, stirring, for 1 minute, then remove and discard the garlic. Add the meat chunks to the skillet a few at a time, turning to brown well on all sides. Do not crowd or they will not brown properly; cook them in batches if necessary. (You may find it easier to do the initial browning in the oven: Preheat to 500°F and roast the meat with 1 tablespoon of the oil and the garlic clove, shaking the pan to turn them once or twice, until brown all over. Remove the garlic clove before continuing.) Season the meat with salt and pepper as it cooks.

2 When the meat is brown, remove it with a slotted spoon. Pour or spoon off most of the fat and turn the heat to medium. Add the onions. Cook, stirring, until they soften, about 10 minutes. Add the flour and cook, stirring, for about 2 minutes. Add the stock or water or wine, bay leaf, thyme, and meat, and bring to a boil. Turn the heat to low and cover. Cook, undisturbed, for 30 minutes.

3 Uncover the pan; the mixture should be quite soupy (if it is not, add a little more liquid). Add the potatoes and carrots, turn the heat up for a minute or so to resume boiling, then lower the heat and cover again. Cook 30 to 60 minutes until the meat and vegetables are tender. Taste for seasoning and add more salt, pepper, and/or thyme if necessary. (If you are not planning to serve the stew immediately, remove the meat and vegetables with a slotted spoon and refrigerate them and the stock separately. Skim the fat from the stock before combining it with the meat and vegetables, reheating, and proceeding with the recipe from this point.)

4 Add the minced garlic and the peas; if you are pleased with the stew's consistency, continue to cook, covered, over low heat. If it is too soupy, remove the cover and raise the heat to high. In either case, cook an additional 5 minutes or so, until the peas have heated through and the garlic flavor has pervaded the stew. Garnish and serve.

Belgian Beef Stew with Beer (Carbonnade) Step 1 remains the same. In Step 2, omit the flour. Use 1 1/2 cups good dark beer for the liquid. Omit the potatoes, carrots, peas, and minced garlic, but otherwise follow the procedure as outlined to the left. This is good finished with a tablespoon of Dijon mustard and served over buttered noodles or with plain boiled potatoes.

Spicy Braised Beef with Lime In Step 1, use peanut oil if you have it. In Step 2, omit bay leaf and thyme and add 1 tablespoon minced garlic, 2 or 3 small dried hot red chiles (or to taste), and the minced peel of 1 lime; use only 1 1/2 cups of liquid. Do not add vegetables. When the meat is tender, finish the dish by adding additional minced garlic and the juice of 1 or 2 limes, to taste. Garnish with minced cilantro leaves.

Beef Stew with Bacon In Step 1, cut 1/4 pound of bacon (preferably slab) into small cubes and cook it over medium heat, stirring, until crisp. Remove with a slotted spoon and reserve. Proceed with the recipe, browning the meat in the bacon fat. Stir in the bacon cubes a minute before serving.

Lamb Stew with Potatoes

The basic lamb stew commonly known as "Irish stew" combines potatoes, onions, meat, and water; browning is unnecessary. Nearly every other lamb stew is just a step away from this one. If you have a lot of parsley, add 2 cups of it, chopped, with the potatoes in Step 2.

Makes 4 to 6 servings

Time: About 2 hours, largely unattended

---

3 pounds waxy red or white potatoes, peeled

2 pounds boneless lamb shoulder, trimmed of excess fat and cut into 2-inch cubes, or 3 to 4 pounds bone-in shoulder or neck, cut into roughly 2-inch chunks

3 cups sliced onions

Salt and freshly ground black pepper to taste

2 to 3 cups liquid: any combination of water, red wine, Full-Flavored Chicken Stock (page 20), store-bought chicken, beef, or vegetable broth, or lamb stock made from extra bones

Minced fresh parsley leaves for garnish

1 Preheat the oven to 350°F. (You can also cook this on the stove if you prefer.) Cut the potatoes into ¼-inch-thick slices and set half of them aside in a bowl of cold salted water. In a large pot or casserole with a cover, combine the lamb, remaining potatoes, onions, salt, and pepper. Add about 2 cups of the liquid to the casserole.

2 Cover the pot, bring it almost to a boil over high heat, then either turn the heat to low or place the stew in the oven. Adjust the heat so the lamb bubbles gently. After the lamb has cooked for about 45 minutes, add the remaining potatoes and more liquid if the mixture seems dry or if you like your stew on the soupy side. Cook until the lamb is tender and the second batch of potatoes is tender but not mushy, another 30 to 60 minutes. Garnish and serve.

Shopping Tips: The lamb shoulder is a cut suitable for roasting, but because of its higher fat content it is not a good grilling cut. In fact, I think its fattiness makes the shoulder (and the nearby neck) best for cooking it with liquid. And, although some people braise lamb shoulder whole, I think it makes more sense to cut it up for a stew; this makes it much easier to discard excess fat and to reduce the cooking time as well.

Lamb shoulders are sold whole or in pieces, with the bone in or out; boneless shoulders, obviously, are much easier to cut into chunks.

Preparation Tips: Discard as much of the hard lamb fat as you can when trimming the meat.

If there is any way you can prepare the stew a day before eating it, do: The flavor will deepen, and you can skim excess fat from the surface. Lamb stew freezes perfectly, so don't worry about making it a week in advance, or about doubling these recipes.

Lamb Stew with Lentils In Step 1, omit the potatoes and cut the amount of onions in half; add 2 cups dried lentils, and 3 cups liquid. In Step 2, add 1 teaspoon minced garlic, 1/2 cup peeled and minced carrots, 1/2 cup minced celery, and 1 cup cored and chopped tomatoes (canned are fine; drain them first). Add more liquid if necessary and cook as above.

Lamb Stew with Dill and Root Vegetables In Step 1, omit the potatoes and cut the amount of onions in half. In Step 2, add about 3 pounds of any combination of root vegetables—such as potatoes, carrots, turnips, and parsnips—all peeled and cut into 1- to 1½-inch chunks. Strip the feathery leaves from a bunch of dill and reserve; tie the stems together and place them in the stew. When the lamb is ready, remove the dill stems. Chop the remaining dill and add all but 1 tablespoon to the stew; stir once, taste for salt and pepper, add a little lemon juice, and taste again, adding more lemon juice if necessary. Garnish with the remaining dill (do not use parsley) and serve immediately.

Lamb Stew with Cabbage and Tomatoes In Step 1, omit the potatoes and cut the amount of onions in half; add 4 cups cored and shredded savoy or green head cabbage, 1 cup peeled and chopped carrots, and 1 tablespoon minced garlic. Add 2 cups cored and chopped tomatoes (canned are fine) and 1 cup liquid (the canned tomato liquid is perfect). Cook as in Step 2, checking and adding more liquid if necessary after 45 minutes. Garnish with minced parsley before serving.

Lamb Shanks with Tomatoes and Olives

Lamb shanks are special because they're cheap and delicious; braise some on a cold winter night, open a bottle of red wine, and relax. Good cured olives make this dish; I like a mixture of the big green kind from southern Italy and kalamatas or another flavorful black variety, but use what you can get.

Makes 4 servings

Time: 2 hours or more, largely unattended

---

1 tablespoon olive oil

4 lamb shanks, about 1 pound each

Salt and freshly ground black pepper to taste

2 cups sliced onions

1 tablespoon minced garlic

1/2 teaspoon fresh thyme leaves, a couple sprigs fresh thyme, or 1/2 teaspoon dried thyme

1/2 cup Full-Flavored Chicken Stock (page 20), store-bought chicken, beef, or vegetable broth, white or red wine, water, or a combination

1 cup cored and chopped tomatoes (canned are fine; drain them first)

1 1/2 cups assorted olives, pitted

Minced fresh basil or parsley leaves for garnish

1 Heat the oil over medium-high heat in a large, deep skillet or casserole that can later be covered. Add the shanks and brown on all sides, seasoning with salt and pepper. (You can also do the initial browning in the oven: Preheat to 500°F and roast the lamb shanks [you may omit the oil], turning once or twice, until brown all over.) Remove the lamb and remove and discard all but 2 tablespoons of fat. Cook the onions over medium heat, stirring occasionally, until they soften, about 10 minutes.

2 Add the garlic and thyme and cook another minute, then add the liquid(s), some salt and pepper, and the tomatoes; stir to blend. Return the lamb shanks to the pan, turn them once or twice, cover, and turn the heat to low.

3 Cook for 30 minutes, turn the shanks, and add the olives. Continue to cook for at least another hour, turning occasionally, until the shanks are very tender (a toothpick inserted into them will meet little resistance) and the meat is nearly falling from the bone. (The recipe can be prepared a day or two in advance up to this point; cool, place in a covered container, and refrigerate.) Garnish and serve.

Cooking Tip: Like most meats that take best to braising, lambshanks can be cooked in advance; up to a day or two if you refrigerate them, up to a week or two if you freeze them. Skim excess fat from the top before reheating. You can braise lamb shanks on top of the stove or in the oven.

Lamb Shanks with Onions and Apricots Soak 1/2 cup chopped dried apricots in 1/2 cup port or other sweet wine. Step 1 remains the same. In Step 2, substitute 1/2 teaspoon ground cinnamon for the thyme, omit the tomatoes, and stud each of the shanks with a clove before returning them to the pan. In Step 3, substitute the apricots and their liquid for the olives. Proceed as above, garnishing with parsley.

Sweet Pork with Spicy Soy Sauce

This dish is great hot, but I also like to make it in advance, refrigerate and skim the fat, then slice the meat and use it in one of three ways: reheated, in the sauce; cold, in sandwiches; or added to any stir-fry or noodle dish. All of these preparations are lightning-quick.

Makes 4 to 6 servings

Time: About 1 hour

1 fresh or dried hot chile, or to taste

2 pounds boneless pork, cut from the butt or shoulder, excess fat removed and cut into 1½- to 2-inch chunks

½ cup soy sauce or fish sauce (nuoc mam or nam pla, available at Asian markets)

2 tablespoons sugar

1 cup Full-Flavored Chicken Stock (page 20), store-bought chicken, beef, or vegetable broth, or water

1 tablespoon minced garlic

1 cup thinly sliced onion

2 tablespoons freshly squeezed lime juice

Salt and lots of freshly ground black pepper to taste

1   If you are using a fresh chile, remove the stem and seeds and mince it. If you're using a dried one, simply crumble it. Then combine all ingredients, except for 1 tablespoon of lime juice and the salt and pepper, in a large pot with a cover. If you have the time, let the mixture sit, refrigerated, for up to a day. (If not, that's okay too.)

2   Bring to a boil over medium-high heat, turn the heat to a minimum and cook, covered, stirring every 10 minutes or so, until the pork is tender, less than 1 hour. (The recipe can be prepared a day or two in advance up to this point; cool, place in a covered container, and refrigerate.)

3   Remove the lid, raise the heat, and boil until the liquid is reduced to less than 1 cup. Taste, add plenty of pepper and some salt if necessary; taste again and adjust seasoning with more pepper, chile, or soy sauce. Sprinkle with the remaining lime juice and serve immediately, or refrigerate and use as described above.

7 | Beans and Vegetables

Ⓦ Weekday

W White Bean Puree

Not only a fine substitute for mashed potatoes, but an unexpected, even elegant side dish for any braised meat.

Makes 4 servings

Time: 10 minutes with precooked beans

About 3 cups drained cooked or canned navy or other white beans

1 cup bean cooking liquid, Full-Flavored Chicken Stock (page 20), store-bought chicken, beef, or vegetable broth, or water

3 tablespoons butter

Salt and freshly ground black pepper to taste

Minced fresh parsley leaves for garnish

1 Puree the beans by putting them through a food mill or using a blender; add as much liquid as you need to make a smooth but not watery puree.

2 Place in a covered microwave-proof dish or medium non-stick saucepan along with the butter. Heat gently (in the microwave, a minute at a time, stirring between sessions) until the butter melts and the beans are hot; season with salt and pepper.

3 Garnish and serve very hot.

W **Pureed Beans with Cream** Cook the beans with a sprig of fresh summer savory or chervil, or a teaspoon of dried. Puree them with about 1/2 cup heavy cream instead of bean cooking liquid or stock. Reheat very gently, using only 1 tablespoon butter. Garnish as above.

W **Garlicky Pureed Beans** Puree the beans, while still hot, with 1 teaspoon minced garlic and a few fresh rosemary leaves, or 1/2 teaspoon dried rosemary. Reheat with butter or olive oil. Garnish as above.

Warm Lentils with Bacon

This dish is largely dependent on bacon for its flavor, so use the best you can find. It's also good with kidney or other red beans; cook them as in Basic Beans (page 87) until nearly tender, then drain before adding them to the onion mixture.

Makes 4 servings

Time: About 45 minutes

1 tablespoon olive or other oil

¼ pound slab bacon, more or less, cut into small cubes

1 medium onion, chopped

1 carrot, peeled and diced

1 teaspoon minced garlic

3 to 4 cups Full-Flavored Chicken Stock (page 20), store-bought chicken, beef, or vegetable broth, or water, or use ½ water and ½ red wine

2 cups lentils, washed and picked over

Salt and freshly ground black pepper to taste

1 bay leaf

2 or 3 sprigs fresh thyme or ½ teaspoon dried thyme

About 1 teaspoon red wine vinegar, or to taste

Minced fresh parsley leaves for garnish

1 Place the oil in a medium saucepan and turn the heat to medium. Cook the bacon in the oil, stirring occasionally, until nicely browned, about 10 minutes. Remove the bacon with a slotted spoon and set aside, leaving the fat in the pot.

2 Cook the onion and carrot in the rendered fat over medium heat until the onion softens, about 5 minutes. Stir in the garlic and cook for 1 minute. Add 3 cups of liquid and bring to a boil over medium-high heat. Stir in the lentils, salt and pepper, and the bay leaf and thyme.

3 Cover partially and cook over medium-low heat, stirring occasionally, until the lentils are nice and tender, 30 minutes or more; add additional liquid as needed, but don't let the mixture become too soupy.

4 When the lentils are soft, raise the heat and boil off any excess liquid if necessary. Stir in about 1 teaspoon vinegar; taste and add more if necessary. Remove and discard bay leaf. Stir in the reserved bacon just before serving, then garnish and serve.

Baked Beans

These are traditional baked beans, easy to make and so much more delicious and fine-textured than those from a can. You may be shocked at the difference. In place of white beans, you could use pinto, kidney, or other red or pink beans.

Makes 4 servings

Time: At least 4 hours, largely unattended

---

1 pound navy, pea, or other white beans

1/2 pound salt pork or good slab bacon (optional)

1/2 cup molasses, or to taste

2 teaspoons ground mustard or 2 tablespoons prepared mustard, or to taste

Salt and freshly ground black pepper to taste

1 Cook the beans as in Basic Beans (page 87), but only until they begin to become tender, about 30 minutes.

2 Preheat the oven to 300°F. Cube or slice the salt pork or bacon and place it in the bottom of a bean pot or other deep-sided ovenproof covered pot, such as a Dutch oven. Drain the beans, then mix them with the molasses and mustard. Pour them over the meat. Gently add enough boiling water to cover the beans by about an inch.

3 Bake, uncovered, for about 3 hours, checking occasionally and adding more water if necessary. At the end of 3 hours, taste and adjust seasoning; you may add more salt, sweetener, or mustard.

4 When the beans are very tender, scoop the meat up from the bottom and lay it on top of the beans; raise the heat to 400°F. Cook until the pork browns a bit and the beans are very bubbly, about 10 minutes. (You may repeat this process several times, scooping the meat to the top and browning it; each repetition darkens the color of the dish and adds flavor.) Serve hot.

Shopping Tip: Salt pork is the fat of the pig's sides and belly, simply salted to preserve it. Bacon—usually from the pig's belly—is also salted, but subsequently smoked. Both add richness to baked beans, but salt pork is usually fattier; bacon adds more flavor. (Fatback is the fresh fat from the pig's back, not salted or smoked, so it lends tenderness to meat rather than big flavor. It is often confused with salt pork and is used for foods like Breakfast Sausage, page 5.)

Preparation Tip: Try any of the following to vary the basic baked beans: Add Worcestershire, soy, or Tabasco sauce to taste; add an onion or two, quartered, and/or a few chunks of peeled carrots; or substitute sausage, cut into chunks, for the salt pork or bacon.

Basic Beans

Time: 30 minutes to 2 hours, largely unattended

It's best to precook beans whenever you can because, unfortunately, precise timing is nearly impossible. A small white bean from a recent harvest may cook twice as fast—may be done in 30 minutes, in fact—as one that's been sitting on your shelf for more than a year and may in fact be 2 years old. So allow enough time unless you've cooked beans from the same batch before and can predict cooking time. Cooked beans store well, in their own liquid, in the refrigerator or freezer, and reheat perfectly on the stove top, in the oven, or in a microwave.

Any quantity dried beans, washed and picked over

Salt to taste

1 Place the beans in a large pot with water to cover. Turn the heat to high and bring to a boil; skim the foam if necessary. Turn the heat down so the beans simmer. Cover loosely.

2 Cook, stirring occasionally, until the beans begin to become tender; add about 1 teaspoon salt per $\frac{1}{2}$ pound of beans, or to taste.

3 Continue to cook, stirring gently, until the beans are as tender as you like; add additional water if necessary. Drain and serve, or use in other recipes, or store covered, in their cooking liquid, in the refrigerator (3 days) or freezer (3 months).

Stewed Chickpeas with Chicken

You can make this dish without the chicken—chickpeas with seasoned tomatoes are wonderful by themselves—or substitute vegetables for it, as in the variation.

Makes 4 servings

Time: About 45 minutes with precooked chickpeas

---

4 cups drained cooked or canned chickpeas

2 cups bean cooking liquid, Full-Flavored Chicken Stock (page 20), chicken, beef, or vegetable broth, or water

Salt and freshly ground black pepper to taste

1 tablespoon canola or other neutral oil

2 to 3 pounds chicken parts, preferably leg-thigh pieces separated at the joint, rinsed and well dried, skin removed if desired

1 large onion, chopped

1 celery stalk, chopped

1 carrot, peeled and chopped

1 tablespoon minced garlic

1 teaspoon peeled and minced fresh ginger

1/2 teaspoon ground coriander

1 teaspoon ground cumin

2 cups peeled, seeded, and chopped tomatoes (canned are fine; don't bother to drain)

Minced cilantro or fresh parsley leaves for garnish

1 Preheat the oven to 400°F. Warm the beans in a large pot with the liquid; add salt and pepper. Turn the heat so that the mixture bubbles very slowly.

2 Place the oil in a large, deep skillet and turn the heat to medium-high. Brown the chicken well on all sides for a total of about 15 minutes; season with salt and pepper, transfer the chicken to a roasting pan, and place in the oven.

3 Pour off all but 3 tablespoons of the fat remaining in the skillet. Turn the heat to medium and add the onion, celery, and carrot. Cook, stirring occasionally, until the vegetables are softened, about 10 minutes. Add the garlic, ginger, coriander, cumin, and tomatoes, and cook for 5 minutes more, stirring occasionally and scraping the bottom of the pan to loosen any brown bits. Add the mixture to the simmering beans.

4 When the chicken has cooked for about 15 minutes, check for doneness (the juices will run clear if you make a small cut in the meat near the bone). When it is ready, remove it from the oven. When the vegetables are tender, place the chickpeas and the vegetables on a large, deep platter; top with the chicken, garnish, and serve.

W **Stewed Chickpeas with Vegetables** Omit the chicken. In Step 2, sauté 3 cups cubed, salted eggplant (page 93) or zucchini in 4 tablespoons of olive oil, until tender, 15 to 30 minutes. Remove and proceed to Step 3. Combine chickpeas and their seasonings with the eggplant and/or zucchini and roast for about 10 minutes, or until the mixture is bubbly and its top begins to brown. Garnish and serve.

Beans and Greens

Best with white beans, whether small or large. Cook them until they are just about falling apart; these should be very creamy. With canned beans, this dish takes about 30 minutes to cook—a perfect filling weekday dish.

Makes 4 servings

Time: 1 to 2 hours, largely unattended

½ pound dried white beans, washed and picked over (page 24)

1 medium onion, unpeeled

1 bay leaf

1 clove

Salt and freshly ground black pepper to taste

1½ pounds dark greens, such as kale, collards, mustard, or broccoli raab, well washed and roughly chopped

1 tablespoon minced garlic

4 teaspoons extra-virgin olive oil

1 Place the beans in a large pot with water to cover. Turn the heat to high and bring to a boil.

2 Cut a slit in the onion and insert the bay leaf; insert the clove into the onion as well and put the onion in the pot. Turn the heat down so the beans simmer. Cover loosely.

3 When the beans begin to soften, after about 30 minutes, season with salt and pepper. Continue to cook, stirring occasionally, until the beans are tender but still intact, about 1 hour; add additional water if necessary.

4 Add the greens to the pot and continue to cook until they are tender, 10 to 30 minutes, depending on the thickness of the stems. If you want a soupy mixture, add more water.

5 Remove the onion. Season the stew with additional salt and pepper. About 3 minutes before serving, add the garlic and stir. Spoon the beans and greens into individual bowls and drizzle with olive oil (or see the variation, below). Serve immediately.

Beans and Greens Gratin Cook as above. When you're done, stir in 1 tablespoon olive oil and spread the mixture in a lightly oiled baking dish. Preheat the broiler. Top the mixture with 1 cup bread crumbs. Drizzle with more olive oil to taste. Run under the broiler, about 4 to 6 inches from the heat source, until lightly browned, about 5 minutes. Serve hot or at room temperature.

ⓦ Steamed Artichokes

Artichoke hearts, or bottoms, are the bottom and innermost part of the vegetable, with outer leaves and choke either removed or, in the case of baby artichokes, absent altogether. Although eating the meat on the leaves of a whole artichoke is fun, getting to the incomparably delicious heart is what it's all about. (See the illustration, at right.)

Artichokes can be simmered in water to cover but they tend to become a bit soggy. It's best to steam them; just make sure that the pot doesn't boil dry. Serve artichokes hot with melted butter, at room temperature with vinaigrette (see page 19), or cold with mayonnaise. Or serve at any temperature with lemon and/or salt.

Makes 4 servings

Time: 45 minutes

---

4 large or 12 very small artichokes

Several sprigs fresh tarragon or thyme (optional)

Salt and freshly ground black pepper to taste

1 With scissors or a large knife, trim the top $\frac{1}{2}$ inch or so from the artichokes. Using a paring knife, peel around the base and cut off the bottom $\frac{1}{4}$ inch. Break off the roughest of the exterior leaves.

2 Place bottom up in a steamer, adding herbs if you like. Cover and cook 20 to 40 minutes. Sample an outer leaf; when it pulls away easily and its meat is tender, the artichokes are done.

3 Drain them upside down for a minute or two longer before serving hot; store upside down (in a covered container) if you plan to serve them later.

Shopping Tip: Artichokes are available year-round, but are most plentiful and cheapest in the spring, when they're in season in the big growing areas of California. Size is irrelevant; any artichoke can be delicious, although large specimens are sometimes woody, so make sure big artichokes feel heavy for their size. Freshness, however, is important: A good artichoke will feel plump and squeak (really) when you squeeze it; the outer leaves will snap off crisply. Store refrigerated, in the vegetable bin. Use as soon as possible.

Preparation Tips: I like to cut the pointed tips from artichoke leaves before cooking, but this is optional; use scissors or a heavy knife to do this.

Artichokes contain an enzyme that makes them discolor as soon as they're cut and cooked; if this bothers you—it doesn't affect the flavor—drop them into a mixture of 1 tablespoon of lemon juice or vinegar per cup of water as you prepare them, and add a splash of vinegar or lemon juice to the cooking water. It's also best to use non-aluminum knives and cooking utensils when working with artichokes.

Trimming Artichokes

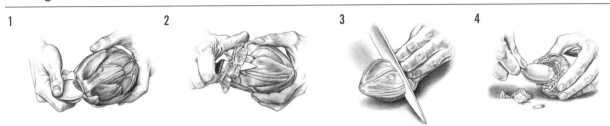

| 1 | 2 | 3 | 4 |

(Step 1) Peel off tough outer leaves. **(Step 2)** Trim around the bottom of the artichoke. **(Step 3)** If you only want to cook the bottom, cut off the top half of the leaves. **(Step 4)** Then scoop out the choke. If you want to leave the artichoke whole but remove the choke, leave it whole and force the top leaves open, then use a long spoon to scrape out the choke.

Collards or Kale, Brazilian-Style

There's only one trick to cooking collards and kale: Make sure you cook them long enough to soften the stems. Undercooked stems are unpleasantly tough and chewy. (One sure way to prevent this is to avoid collards with stems more than ¹/₈ inch thick.) "Brazilian-Style" sounds exotic, but this is actually a deliciously simple way to prepare greens.

Makes 4 servings

Time: 15 minutes

1½ pounds young collards or kale, or other dark green, washed and very well dried

3 tablespoons olive or peanut oil

1 tablespoon minced garlic

Salt and freshly ground black pepper to taste

¼ to ¹/₃ cup freshly squeezed lemon juice or red or white wine vinegar

Preparing Collards and Kale

Remove and discard the stems if they are very thick (or remove them and cook them a little longer than the leaves). Cut on either side of them, at an angle.

The easiest way to chop large leaves is to roll them up and cut across the log.

1 Chop the greens into fairly small pieces; no dimension should be more than 2 inches.

2 Meanwhile, heat a 12-inch skillet or wok over high heat until smoking. Add the oil to the skillet, let sit for a few seconds, then toss in the greens and the garlic.

3 Cook over high heat, stirring almost constantly, until the greens wilt and begin to brown, 3 to 8 minutes (depending largely on the power of your burner).

4 Season with salt and pepper and add a little lemon juice or vinegar. Taste, adjust seasoning, and serve immediately.

Shopping Tip: Look for collards or kale with dark-green color and firm, unwilted leaves. Young, small leaves with stems no thicker than a pencil will be easier to clean, be less wasteful, and cook more quickly. They will also have a better texture when cooked. Collards are sold year-round, but are best in the late fall. These are sturdy greens that keep well, especially if you wrap them in plastic. They are unlikely to rot, but will begin to turn yellow after a few days; try to use them before that happens.

Preparation Tip: If the stems are thick, strip the leaves, chop the stems, and start cooking the stems a couple of minutes before the leaves. (See illustration at left.)

Grilled or Broiled Eggplant Slices

This is the simplest way to prepare eggplant, and it makes a delicious side dish.

Makes 4 servings

Time: 20 minutes, plus time to preheat the grill and salt the eggplant

---

1 medium-to-large eggplant
(1 to 1½ pounds)

1 teaspoon minced garlic (optional)

4 to 6 tablespoons olive oil

Salt and freshly ground black pepper to taste

Minced fresh parsley leaves for garnish

1 Peel the eggplant if the skin is thick or the eggplant is less than perfectly firm. Cut it into ½-inch-thick slices and salt it if you like (see Tip below). Start a charcoal or wood fire or preheat a gas grill or broiler; the rack should be 4 to 6 inches from the heat source.

2 Stir the optional garlic into the olive oil, then brush one side of the eggplant slices with the oil. Place, oiled side down, on a baking sheet or directly on the grill. Sprinkle with salt (if you salted the eggplant, hold off) and pepper, then brush with more oil.

3 Broil or grill until browned on both sides, turning once or twice and brushing with more oil if the eggplant looks dry. Serve hot or at room temperature, garnished with parsley.

Shopping Tip: Eggplant must be firm; like cucumber, the length is not so important, but the width is. Long, narrow eggplant tend to contain few seeds. Big, fleshy eggplant usually contain more seeds and become softer more readily. Store eggplant in the refrigerator, and use it as soon as you can; although the outside will not look much different, the inside will become soft and bitter within a few days.

Preparation Tip: Salting larger eggplant draws out excess moisture and a certain amount of bitterness along with it. Trim off the ends, then cut it into slices (you can cut long slices or crosswise ones) from ½ to 1 inch thick. Or cut it into chunks. Sprinkle both sides of the slices (or all sides of the chunks) liberally with coarse salt, then let drain in a colander for at least half an hour, or up to 2 hours. Rinse and squeeze dry between paper or cloth towels.

Grilled or Broiled Eggplant Slices with Miso Dressing Use canola or other neutral oil in place of olive oil, and omit the garlic. Broil or grill the eggplant, and serve with a dressing made by mixing together 4 tablespoons miso; 1 teaspoon sugar; 1 tablespoon mirin (or ½ tablespoon honey, thinned with water); and rice or other mild vinegar to taste.

Braised Endive, Escarole, or Radicchio with Prosciutto

Belgian endive, the small red head that is radicchio, and the lettuce-like head that is generally called escarole are all part of a confusing cluster of vegetables. They are all chicory, or closely related to chicory; the differences are more in form and cultivation (Belgian endive is the neat-looking cluster of leaves grown from the chicory root, but in the dark—which keeps it nearly white) than in flavor or handling. Since they're all quite bitter, firm, and fleshy, they're as good cooked as they are raw.

Endive, with its neat little shape, is perfect for braising, but escarole and radicchio taste just as good.

Makes 4 servings

Time: About 1 hour

1 tablespoon olive oil

4 Belgian endives, trimmed at the base, damaged leaves removed, or about 1 pound of escarole or radicchio, cleaned and roughly chopped

¼ cup minced prosciutto or other dry-cured ham

½ cup Full-Flavored Chicken Stock (page 20), store-bought chicken, beef, or vegetable broth, or water

Salt and freshly ground black pepper to taste

1 teaspoon freshly squeezed lemon juice or white wine vinegar

1 Heat the olive oil over medium heat in a medium to large non-stick skillet that can later be covered. Add the endives and cook, turning once or twice, until they begin to brown.

2 Add the prosciutto or ham, stock or water, salt, and pepper. Cover and cook over the lowest possible heat, turning occasionally, until very tender, about 45 minutes. Uncover and turn the heat up a bit to evaporate any remaining liquid.

3 Drizzle with lemon juice or vinegar and serve.

Shopping Tip: All chicories, including Belgian endive, are crops of the late fall and winter, and can be found when other interesting salad greens are scarce. Buy firm, fleshy specimens, and store, lightly wrapped, in the vegetable bin. Belgian endive is considered best if it is nearly white; it turns green when exposed to light, and becomes a little more bitter. All of these keep better than most salad greens—up to a week—but are still best when used as soon as possible.

Cooking Tip: Endive, escarole, and radicchio are done when crisp-tender; if you let them cook until they are completely tender, mushiness is the inevitable result.

Potato Croquettes

Croquettes are the kinds of things that people used to make on weekdays, but no one has the time now. Yet these crisp, creamy, old-fashioned morsels are fun to make and great to eat.

Makes 4 to 6 servings

Time: 1 hour or less

1½ pounds baking potatoes, such as Idaho or Russet, prepared as for Mashed Potatoes (at right) but without the butter

2 eggs

Pinch freshly grated nutmeg

2 tablespoons minced fresh parsley leaves, plus more for garnish

½ cup freshly grated Parmesan cheese

Salt and freshly ground black pepper to taste

Flour as needed

Olive oil or butter as needed

Plain bread crumbs for dredging

1 Combine the potatoes, eggs, nutmeg, 2 tablespoons parsley, Parmesan, salt, and pepper. Add enough flour (you may not need any) to allow the potatoes to hold their shape; mold into hamburger-shaped cakes. If time allows, refrigerate for about 1 hour.

2 Place the oil or butter in a large, deep skillet and turn the heat to medium-high. When the butter melts or the oil becomes hot, dredge the cakes in bread crumbs and place in the pan. Cook until brown on one side, about 5 minutes. Turn and brown the other side. Garnish and serve hot or at room temperature.

Shopping Tips: Starchy potatoes, often called Idaho or Russet, make the best mashed and baked potatoes and good french fries. I call these "baking potatoes, such as Idaho or Russet."

All potatoes should be quite firm when you buy them. Look out for damaged potatoes, those with mold or soft spots, those that are flabby, those with sprouts, or those with green spots. Store potatoes in a cool, dark place, but not in the refrigerator (low-starch potatoes can be refrigerated, however).

Ⓦ Mashed Potatoes

Makes 4 servings • Time: About 40 minutes

If you like mashed potatoes lumpy, mash them with a fork or potato masher; if you like them creamy, use a food mill or ricer.

2 pounds baking potatoes, such as Idaho or Russet, peeled and cut into quarters

3 tablespoons butter

¾ cup milk, gently warmed

Salt and freshly ground black pepper to taste

Boil potatoes in a pot with salted water to cover, until soft, about 30 minutes. When the potatoes are done, drain them, then mash them well or put them through a food mill. Return them to the pot over very low heat and stir in the butter and—gradually—the milk, beating with a wooden spoon until smooth and creamy. Season with salt and pepper. Serve, keep warm, or reheat in a microwave.

Marinated Roasted, Grilled, or Broiled Peppers

There are many techniques for "roasting" peppers; all work. These are the three easiest and neatest.

Makes 4 servings

Time: About 1 hour, plus marinating time and time to preheat the grill

---

4 red or yellow bell peppers, rinsed

¼ cup extra-virgin olive oil

1 clove garlic, crushed

1 tablespoon balsamic, sherry, or other flavorful vinegar

Salt and freshly ground black pepper to taste

Minced fresh basil, oregano, or parsley leaves for garnish

1 To roast the peppers, preheat the oven to 500°F. Put the peppers in a roasting pan and place in the oven, with the rack set near the top. Roast, shaking the pan frequently, until the peppers shrivel and collapse, 30 to 40 minutes. Proceed to Step 2.

To grill the peppers, start a charcoal or wood fire or preheat a gas grill; the fire should be quite hot. Place the peppers on the grill (cover the grill if possible) and cook, turning occasionally, and taking care not to let the peppers burn too badly (some blackening is not only okay, it's desirable), until the peppers collapse, 10 to 20 minutes total. Proceed to Step 2.

To broil the peppers, preheat the broiler. Place the peppers in a roasting pan and set under the broiler, about 4 inches from the heat source. Broil, turning as each side browns and taking care not to let the peppers burn too badly (some blackening is not only okay, it's desirable), until the peppers shrivel and collapse, 10 to 20 minutes total. Proceed to Step 2.

2 Place the hot peppers in a bowl and cover with plastic wrap. Let cool, then peel, discarding skins, seeds, and stems.

3 Combine the oil, garlic, vinegar, salt, and pepper and marinate the peppers in this mixture, from 1 to 24 hours. Serve at room temperature, garnished with minced herb.

Shopping Tip: Yellow and orange peppers seem to be mellowest, but they're usually expensive, so red is the common first choice, green a distant last. Avoid peppers with soft spots or bruises, or those that feel very full—don't pay (by weight) for lots of seeds. Store peppers, unwrapped, in the vegetable bin, for a week or so.

Preparation Tip: Peppers should always be cored and stemmed before cooking unless, of course, you're roasting or grilling them whole, as in this recipe. If you plan to cut the peppers into strips, or dice them, just start by cutting them in half; remove the cap and seed mass with your fingers. Alternatively, you can cut a circle around the cap and pull it off, along with most of the seeds; rinse out the remaining seeds. Peppers can also be peeled with a vegetable peeler, an added refinement that doesn't take long and removes an element of bitterness.

Braised Butternut or Other Winter Squash with Garlic

These are long-keeping squashes that have much in common with pumpkin and sweet potato: yellow to orange flesh, usually quite sweet and creamy when cooked. This is one of those dishes whose wonderful flavor belies its simplicity.

Makes 4 servings

Time: About 30 minutes

2 tablespoons olive oil

1 tablespoon minced garlic

1½ pounds butternut or other winter squash, peeled, and cut into ½- to 1-inch cubes

¼ cup Full-Flavored Chicken Stock (page 20), store-bought chicken, beef, or vegetable broth, or water

Salt and freshly ground black pepper to taste

Minced fresh parsley leaves for garnish

1 Place the olive oil and garlic in a large, deep skillet and turn the heat to medium. When the garlic begins to color, add the squash, stock or water, salt, and pepper. Bring to a boil, cover, and turn the heat to low. Cook, stirring once or twice, until the squash is tender, about 15 minutes.

2 Uncover the pan and turn the heat to medium-high. Cook, shaking the pan occasionally and stirring somewhat less often, until all the liquid is evaporated and the squash has begun to brown, 5 to 10 minutes. Turn the heat to low and cook until the squash is as browned and crisp as you like.

3 Taste and adjust seasoning, garnish, and serve.

Shopping Tip: Winter squash should be firm, with no soft spots or obvious damage. It's in season from late summer through winter, although it keeps so well that there are almost always some for sale. Store as you would potatoes, in a cool, dry place, but not in the refrigerator. Use within a month.

Preparation Tips: The most difficult thing about winter squash is peeling it—even the smooth-skinned varieties, such as butternut, can defeat many peelers. (Use a paring knife and be careful.) For acorn and other bumpy squash, you have no choice but to cook with the skin still on.

Use a cleaver or very large knife to split hard squash in half. Scoop out the seeds and strings and discard.

Cooking Tip: It's done when very tender. If you're cooking with liquid, make sure it doesn't become waterlogged. If you're roasting or sautéing, it's difficult to overcook.

Grilled Mixed Vegetables

This is a "for instance" recipe. You can grill almost any vegetable, as long as you slice it into 1/2-inch-thick (or slightly thinner) slices. Soft vegetables, such as zucchini, can be made thicker. Very hard vegetables, such as potatoes (always use waxy red or white potatoes for grilling), are best parboiled until nearly tender before grilling.

Makes 4 to 6 servings

Time: 45 minutes, plus time to preheat the grill

---

1 Spanish or other large onion

2 red or yellow bell peppers, stemmed, halved, and seeded

1 eggplant, cut into 1/2-inch-thick slices and salted (page 93) if time allows

1 zucchini, cut lengthwise into 1/2-inch-thick slices

Extra-virgin olive oil as needed

Salt and freshly ground black pepper to taste

chopped fresh basil

1 Start a charcoal or wood fire or preheat a gas grill. Cut the root and flower end from the onion so that it will sit flat on the grill. Then cut it in half, through its equator. Prepare the other vegetables.

2 Brush all of the vegetables liberally with olive oil and sprinkle with salt and pepper. Grill, turning once or twice, until nicely browned on both sides and tender throughout, about 15 minutes. Drizzle with a little more olive oil and sprinkle with the chopped basil, and serve hot or at room temperature.

Oven-Baked Ratatouille

This is a mixture of soft vegetables called *tian*, gently baked in layers until very tender. If you have good olive oil and fresh herbs, this will be sensational.

Makes 4 servings

Time: About 1¼ hours

---

10 cloves garlic

2 large onions, thinly sliced

2 large eggplant, about 2 pounds total, sliced ½-inch thick and salted if time allows (page 93)

4 red or yellow bell peppers, stemmed, peeled if desired, seeded, and sliced into 3 or 4 pieces each

4 ripe red tomatoes, cored, skins and seeds removed, and cut into thick slices

1 teaspoon fresh thyme, rosemary, or savory leaves

Salt and freshly ground black pepper to taste

½ cup extra-virgin olive oil

2 tablespoons minced fresh parsley, basil, or chervil leaves for garnish

1 Preheat the oven to 350°F.

2 Either of these techniques will make the garlic easier to peel: Drop it into boiling water; leave it there for 30 seconds, then remove it. Or toast it in a dry skillet over medium heat, shaking frequently, for 3 or 4 minutes. Peel and cut each clove in half.

3 In a casserole, make a layer of onion, followed by one of eggplant, peppers, tomatoes, herbs, salt, pepper, and garlic cloves. Repeat. Drizzle the ratatouille with the olive oil and place in the oven. Bake for about an hour, pressing down on the vegetables occasionally, until they are all completely tender. Garnish and serve, hot or at room temperature.

8 | Desserts

Summer Pudding

You can use pound cake (even frozen pound cake is okay) instead of bread here for extra flavor. But you cannot use frozen berries; fresh ones are essential (that's why it's "summer" pudding). Keep all the berries whole, except for strawberries, which should be sliced. For a delicious finishing touch, serve with whipped cream.

Makes 4 to 6 servings

Time: 20 minutes, plus chilling time

---

4 cups mixed berries: whole blackberries, raspberries, blueberries, currants, and strawberries; the raspberries held aside

About 1 cup water

½ cup sugar, or more as needed

Unsalted butter as needed

6 to 8 slices good white bread, crusts removed

1 In a large saucepan, combine all the berries except the raspberries with about 1 cup of water and the ½ cup sugar; turn the heat to medium. Cook, stirring occasionally, until the berries fall apart, 10 to 15 minutes. Stir in the raspberries. Taste and add more sugar if needed; pass through a sieve to remove seeds and skins.

2 Meanwhile, butter the bread and the bottom and sides of an 8-cup soufflé, gratin, or other dish; sprinkle the bottom of the dish lightly with sugar. Put half the bread in the bottom of the dish. Cover with half the berry mixture, then repeat the layers.

3 Cover with a plate that fits into the dish, and weight the plate so it presses down on the mixture. Refrigerate for several hours or overnight. Unmold if you like, or serve straight from the dish.

Panna Cotta

An Italian eggless custard, thickened with gelatin and flavored with nothing but vanilla.

Makes 6 servings

Time: About 30 minutes, plus time to chill

---

1 cup milk

1 (1/4 ounce) package unflavored gelatin

1 vanilla bean

2 cups heavy cream

1/2 cup sugar

An assortment of berries, or raspberry sauce (see Raspberry, Strawberry, or Other Fruit Sauce, at right) (optional)

Handling Vanilla Beans

1

2

(Step 1) To use a vanilla bean, split it in half the long way. **(Step 2)** Scrape out the seeds. Reserve the pod for vanilla sugar.

1 Place 1/2 cup of the milk in a medium saucepan and sprinkle the gelatin over it; let sit for 5 minutes. Turn the heat to low and cook, stirring, until the gelatin dissolves completely.

2 Cut the vanilla bean in half, lengthwise. Scrape out seeds; add both seeds and pod to the pot, along with the remaining milk, cream, and sugar. Cook over medium heat, stirring, until steam rises from the pot. Turn off the heat, cover, and let steep for 15 to 30 minutes.

3 Remove the vanilla pod and pour the mixture into six custard cups. Chill until set. Serve in the cups, or dip the cups in hot water for about 10 seconds each, then invert onto plates. Serve, the same day you make it, with berries or sauce if you like.

Ⓦ Raspberry, Strawberry, or Other Fruit Sauce
Makes about 2 cups • Time: 5 to 10 minutes

This is an easy way to make a fruit sauce, particularly with soft fruits and berries. You get pure, straightforward flavor, and a very saucy consistency.

2 cups any berries or other soft ripe fruit: peaches, cherries, nectarines, mangoes, etc., picked over, pitted, peeled, washed, and/or dried, as necessary

Confectioners' sugar to taste

A little orange juice, freshly squeezed lemon juice, or fruity white wine (optional)

1 Puree the fruit in a blender; if you have used raspberries or blackberries, put the puree through a sieve to remove the seeds.

2 Combine with confectioners' sugar to taste. If necessary, thin with a little water, or use orange juice, lemon juice, or fruity white wine. Use immediately or refrigerate for a day or two.

Chocolate Mousse

Once thought of as the most elegant of desserts, this ultra-rich chocolate pudding is still a real winner. It's blazing quick to make—I've prepared it after dinner and still served it before my guests left—which I do early. Once the chocolate is melted, the cooking is over; the mousse just sits until it sets up.

You can spike chocolate mousse with rum, coffee, or other flavorings, but I like it simple—it's the intensity of chocolate that makes it special.

Makes 6 servings

Time: 20 minutes, plus time to chill

---

2 tablespoons unsalted butter

4 ounces bittersweet or semisweet chocolate, chopped

3 eggs, separated

1/4 cup sugar

1/2 cup heavy cream

1/2 teaspoon vanilla extract

1 Use a double boiler or a small saucepan over low heat to melt the butter and chocolate together. Just before the chocolate finishes melting, remove it from the stove and beat with a wooden spoon until smooth.

2 Transfer the chocolate mixture to a bowl and beat in the egg yolks with a whisk. Refrigerate.

3 Beat the egg whites with half the sugar until they hold stiff peaks but are not dry. Set aside. Beat the cream with the remaining sugar and vanilla until it holds soft peaks.

4 Stir a couple of spoonfuls of the whites into the chocolate mixture to lighten it a bit, then fold in the remaining whites thoroughly but gently. Fold in the cream and refrigerate until chilled. If you are in a hurry, divide the mousse among six cups; it will chill much faster. Serve within a day or two of making.

Bread Pudding

An old-fashioned dessert that has deservedly made a comeback. Suitable for both casual and elegant meals, largely because everyone loves it.

Makes 6 servings

Time: About 1 hour, largely unattended

---

3 cups milk

4 tablespoons (1/2 stick) unsalted butter, plus some for greasing the pan

1 1/2 teaspoons ground cinnamon

1/2 cup sugar plus 1 tablespoon

Pinch salt

8 slices white bread, crusts removed if they are very thick

3 eggs

1 Preheat the oven to 350°F. Over low heat in a small saucepan, warm the milk, butter, 1 teaspoon cinnamon, 1/2 cup sugar, and salt, just until the butter melts. Meanwhile, butter a 1 1/2-quart or 8-inch square baking dish (glass is nice), and cut or tear the bread into bite-sized pieces; they need not be too small.

2 Place the bread in the baking dish and pour the hot milk over it. Let it sit for a few minutes, occasionally submerging any pieces of bread that rise to the top. Beat the eggs briefly and stir them into the bread mixture. Mix together the remaining sugar and cinnamon and sprinkle over the top. Set the baking dish in a larger baking pan and pour hot water in, to within about an inch of the top of the dish.

3 Bake 45 minutes to 1 hour, or until a thin-bladed knife inserted in the center comes out clean, or nearly so; the center should be just a little wobbly. Run under the broiler for about 30 seconds if you like, to brown the top a bit. Serve warm or cold, with or without whipped cream. This keeps well for 2 days or more, covered and refrigerated.

Chocolate Bread Pudding In Step 1, melt 2 ounces chopped bittersweet chocolate with the butter and milk. Proceed as above.

Apple-Raisin Bread Pudding Step 1 remains the same. In Step 2, add 1 cup peeled, grated, and drained apples and 1/4 cup or more raisins to the mixture along with the eggs. Proceed as above.

Vanilla Cream Pie

Master this one basic recipe and you can make all the cream pies you've dreamed of. This is an efficient recipe with dazzling results: The cream filling uses only egg yolks, but the egg whites are used in the lofty and sweet meringue topping.

Note that though they're called cream pies, milk is the chosen liquid. But use whole milk if at all possible. If you have only low-fat milk, substitute 1/4 cup of cream for 1/4 cup of the milk, if possible; incongruous, yes, but it will make for a better pie.

Makes about 8 servings

Time: About 1½ hours

---

1 Graham Cracker Crust (at right)

¾ cup sugar

2 tablespoons cornstarch

Pinch salt

3 or 4 eggs, separated

2½ cups whole milk or 2¼ cups low-fat milk mixed with ¼ cup cream

1 vanilla bean or 2 teaspoons vanilla extract

2 tablespoons unsalted butter, softened

Pinch cream of tartar

¼ cup confectioners' sugar

1 Prebake the crust (see Graham Cracker Crust, at right), and start the filling while the crust is in the oven. When the crust is done, set the oven to 350°F and cool the crust slightly on a rack.

2 In a small saucepan, combine the sugar with the cornstarch and salt. Mix together the egg yolks and milk. If you're using a vanilla bean, split it and scrape out the seeds; stir them into the milk mixture (reserve the bean itself to make vanilla sugar). Stir the milk-egg mixture into the sugar-cornstarch mixture over medium heat; at first, whisk occasionally to eliminate lumps. Then stir almost constantly until the mixture boils and thickens, about 10 minutes. Stir in the butter (and vanilla extract, if you're using it) and set aside.

3 Make the meringue: Beat the egg whites with a pinch of salt and cream of tartar, until foamy. Keep beating, gradually adding the confectioners' sugar, until the mixture is shiny and holds fairly stiff peaks.

4 Place the pie plate on a baking sheet. Pour the warm filling into the warm crust. Cover with the meringue, making sure the meringue comes in contact with the edges of the crust. Note that the meringue will hold its shape, so you can decorate it if you like. Bake until the meringue is lightly browned, 10 to 15 minutes. Cool on a rack, then refrigerate; serve cool.

Chocolate Cream Pie Add 2 ounces chopped or grated bittersweet or semi-sweet chocolate to the milk mixture as it cooks in Step 2.

Banana Cream Pie Stir 1 cup thinly sliced banana into the thickened cream filling before pouring it into the pie shell in Step 4.

Graham Cracker Crust

For any single-crust pie, 8 to 10 inches in diameter • Time: 20 minutes

Graham cracker crusts, good for cream or meringue pies and cheesecakes, are often prebaked. You can use roughly these same proportions and techniques for any cookie crumb crust—such as vanilla wafers, chocolate cookies, or gingersnaps—although if the cookies contain a great deal of fat you'll want to reduce the amount of butter. If you need a larger crust, simply increase the ingredients proportionally.

To crumble graham crackers, place them in a heavy plastic bag and seal, then roll over the bag as many times as necessary with a rolling pin. Alternatively, break the crackers into the container of a food processor and process until crumbly. (Or buy graham cracker crumbs.)

6 tablespoons unsalted butter

3 tablespoons sugar

**6 ounces broken graham crackers,
about 1½ cups**

1 Gently melt the butter in a small saucepan.

2 Combine sugar with graham cracker crumbs in a bowl or food processor. Slowly add the butter, stirring or processing until well blended. Press the crumbs into the bottom and sides of a 9-inch pie plate.

3 To prebake, heat the oven to 350°F. Bake the crust for 8 to 10 minutes, just until it begins to brown. Cool on a rack before filling; the crust will harden as it cools.

Caramelized Apple Tart (Tarte Tatin)

There is nothing better than Tarte Tatin but, to be at its best, it should be made almost at the last minute. The ideal is to prepare it just before serving the meal and bake it while you're eating.

Makes about 8 servings

Time: About 1 hour

6 Granny Smith or any other tart, hard apple

Juice of ½ lemon

8 tablespoons (1 stick) butter, ut into pieces

¾ cup sugar

1 recipe Rich Tart Crust, chilled but not yet rolled out (at right)

1 Preheat the oven to 400°F.

2 Peel, core, and quarter the apples; toss with the lemon juice. Press the butter into the bottom and sides of a medium, heavy, ovenproof skillet (cast iron is good). Sprinkle the butter with the sugar. Press the apple slices into the sugar, arranging them in concentric circles and making certain to pack them in tightly; they will shrink considerably during cooking.

3 Place the pan over medium-high heat. Cook for 15 to 20 minutes, or until the butter-sugar mixture has turned a very deep, dark brown. While it is cooking, roll out the pastry. When the apples are ready, remove the pan from the heat. Lay the pastry on top of the apples, bringing the dough to the edges of the pan to seal it. Prick the dough with a fork and bake about 20 minutes, or until the pastry is golden brown.

4 Remove the tart from the oven and let it sit for 5 minutes. Shake the hot pan to loosen the apples stuck to the bottom of the skillet. Invert the whole tart onto a large serving dish, taking care not to burn yourself (the juices are hot). Serve immediately or at room temperature.

Peeling and Coring an Apple

For pies and tarts, cut the apple in quarters and remove the core with a melon baller or a paring knife.

Rich Tart Crust

Makes enough for a generous 10-inch tart • Time: 10 minutes

Egg yolks and a little extra butter enrich this crust, giving it more flavor and body than a typical pie crust. In fact, it's like a great big cookie.

1½ cups (about 7 ounces) all-purpose flour, plus more as needed

½ teaspoon salt

2 tablespoons sugar

10 tablespoons (1¼ sticks) cold unsalted butter, cut into about 10 pieces

2 egg yolks, plus more as needed

3 tablespoons ice water, plus 1 tablespoon if needed

1 Combine the flour, salt, and sugar in the container of a food processor; pulse once or twice. Add the butter and turn on the machine; process until the butter and flour are blended and the mixture looks like cornmeal, about 10 seconds. Add the egg yolks and process another few seconds.

2 Place the mixture in a bowl and sprinkle 3 tablespoons of water over it. Use a wooden spoon or a rubber spatula to gradually gather the mixture into a ball; if the mixture is dry, add another tablespoon of ice water. When you can make the mixture into a ball with your hands, do so. Wrap in plastic, flatten into a small disk, and freeze the dough for 10 minutes (or refrigerate for 30 minutes); this will ease rolling. (You can also refrigerate the dough for a day or two, or freeze it almost indefinitely.)

3 You can roll the dough between two sheets of plastic wrap, usually quite successfully; sprinkle both sides of it with a little more flour, then proceed. Or sprinkle a countertop or large board with flour. Unwrap the dough and place it on the work surface; sprinkle its top with flour. If the dough is hard, let it rest for a few minutes; it should give a little when you press your fingers into it.

4 Roll with light pressure, from the center out. If the dough seems very sticky at first, add a little flour; but if it becomes sticky while you're rolling, return it to the refrigerator for 10 minutes before proceeding. Continue to roll, adding flour as necessary, rotating the dough occasionally, and turning it over once or twice. (Use ragged edges of dough to repair any tears, adding a drop of water while you press the patch into place.) When the diameter of the dough is equal to that of the tart, cover the apples as described in the recipe to the left.

Single-Layer Butter Cake

This is my favorite "plain" cake, a purebred of all the essential ingredients in the right proportions. It can be served plain, with a little confectioners' sugar, or with some fruit salad. Or you can split, fill, and top it with whipped cream, jam, any icing, or the delicious chocolate glaze provided here.

Cakes have a way of showcasing off-flavors: If any ingredient is stale (or worse, rancid), or even second-rate, that flavor will somehow pop to the fore. Use high-quality butter, eggs, chocolate, nuts, and extracts for the best cakes.

Makes at least 8 servings

Time: About 1 hour

---

12 tablespoons (1½ sticks) unsalted butter, softened, plus butter for greasing the pan and paper

Flour for dusting the pan

1¼ cups sugar

6 eggs

½ pound blanched almonds

Grated or minced zest of 1 lemon or orange, or more if you like

1 Preheat the oven to 350°F. Butter the bottom and sides of a 2-inch-deep 10-inch cake or springform pan; cover the bottom with a circle of waxed or parchment paper, butter the paper, and sift flour over the whole pan; invert to remove the excess flour.

2 Use an electric mixer to cream the butter and ¼ cup of the sugar. Separate 3 of the eggs and reserve the whites. Beat in the yolks one at a time, until the mixture is light in color.

3 Grind the nuts in a food processor until they are the consistency of meal. Mix them with ¾ cup of the sugar and the lemon zest. Beat in 3 whole eggs, one at a time, blending well.

4 Beat the egg whites; when they are foamy, gradually beat in the remaining ¼ cup sugar, until the mixture holds a soft peak. Combine the butter and nut mixtures and stir. Gently fold in the beaten egg whites and pour into the pan.

5 Bake for about 30 minutes, or until a toothpick inserted into the center of the cake comes out clean. Let cool for 10 minutes, then unmold. This keeps fairly well for a day or two, wrapped in waxed paper.

Dark Chocolate Glaze

Makes enough to cover 1 (9-inch) layer cake • Time: 10 minutes

This is a perfect finish for cakes and cupcakes. It's bittersweet and rich, very intense, but you don't use that much; it isn't a filling, just a glaze. Apply it while it's hot, with an oiled spatula, on a chilled cake; it will solidify perfectly and almost instantly.

¾ cup top-quality unsweetened cocoa powder

½ cup heavy cream

6 tablespoons (¾ stick) unsalted butter, cut into bits

¾ cup confectioners' sugar

Tiny pinch salt

½ teaspoon vanilla extract

1 Mix together the cocoa, cream, butter, confectioners' sugar, and salt in a small saucepan. Cook over low heat until combined and thickened, 5 to 10 minutes.

2 Stir in the vanilla and use immediately.

Lemon Cheesecake with Sour Cream Topping

Most veteran cooks have their favorite cheesecake, and this is mine. It's relatively low in sugar, and the lemon provides balance. You can skip the sour cream topping if you feel that enough is enough.

Makes at least 12 servings

Time: About 1½ hours

Unsalted butter for greasing the pan

1 double recipe Graham Cracker Crust (page 107)

4 eggs, separated

24 ounces (3 [8-ounce] packages) cream cheese

Grated zest and juice of 1 lemon

1 cup sugar, plus 1 tablespoon (optional)

1 tablespoon all-purpose flour

2 cups sour cream (optional)

1 teaspoon vanilla extract (optional)

1 Liberally butter a 9- or 10-inch springform pan, then press the crust into its bottom. Preheat the oven to 325°F.

2 Use an electric mixer to beat the egg yolks until light; add the cheese, lemon zest and juice, and 1 cup of the sugar and beat until smooth. Stir in the flour.

3 Beat the egg whites until they hold soft peaks; use a rubber spatula or your hand to fold them into the yolk-cheese mixture gently but thoroughly. Turn the batter into the prepared pan and place the pan in a baking pan large enough to hold it comfortably. Add warm water to the baking pan, so that it comes to within an inch of the top of the springform pan (see Tips below). Transfer carefully to the oven and bake until the cake is just set and very lightly browned, about an hour. Turn the oven up to 450°F if you're making the sour cream topping.

4 Remove the cake from the oven and cool completely if not adding the sour cream topping. If you're making the topping, combine the sour cream with the vanilla and the optional 1 tablespoon sugar and spread on the top of the cake. Return it to the oven for 10 minutes, without the water bath; turn off the oven and let the cake cool for 30 minutes before removing it. Cool on a rack, cover with plastic wrap, then refrigerate until well chilled before slicing and serving. This will keep in good shape for several days.

Preparation Tips: Before you use a springform pan, make sure that your springform pan is watertight. (Close it and add water; as long as it doesn't leak, you're okay.)

Although it is not always essential, it helps to cook cheesecakes (and custards) in a water bath, which is no more than a pan of water into which you place the baking pan. By moderating the temperature around the cheesecake, the water bath (also called a bain-marie) makes for more even cooking.

Biscotti

These double-baked cookies can be simple or dressed up. Either way they are great with coffee and simple and elegant enough to be the only dessert with a special meal. Biscotti can be made with no butter at all, which makes them extra crunchy. Butter, however, adds tenderness and flavor, and I prefer them that way.

Makes 3 to 4 dozen

Time: About 1¼ hours

___

4 tablespoons (½ stick) unsalted butter, softened, plus more for greasing the baking sheets

¾ cup sugar

2 eggs

½ teaspoon vanilla or almond extract

2¼ cups (about 10 ounces) all-purpose flour, plus more for dusting the baking sheets

2 teaspoons baking powder

Pinch salt

___

3 Simple Ideas for Biscotti

1 Stir 1 cup slivered blanched almonds, toasted and chopped hazelnuts, or other chopped nuts into prepared dough before baking.

2 Mix 1 teaspoon minced lemon zest or orange zest into the dry ingredients.

3 Melt 8 ounces semisweet chocolate with 3 tablespoons unsalted butter. Spread this mixture onto one side of the biscotti when they are done. Cool on rack until chocolate coating is firm.

1 Preheat the oven to 375°F. Use an electric mixer to cream together the butter and the sugar until light and fluffy; beat in the eggs, one at a time, then the vanilla or almond extract.

2 Mix the flour, baking powder, and salt in a bowl, and add it to the batter a little at a time.

3 Butter two baking sheets and dust them with flour; invert the sheets and tap them to remove excess flour. Divide the dough in half and shape each half into a 2-inch-wide log. Place each log onto one of the baking sheets.

4 Bake until the loaves are golden and beginning to crack on top, about 30 minutes; remove the logs from the oven. Lower the oven temperature to 250°F.

5 When the loaves are cool enough to handle, cut each on the diagonal into ½-inch-thick slices, using a serrated knife. Place the slices on the sheets, return to the oven, and leave them there until they dry out, about 15 to 20 minutes; turn once. Cool on wire racks. These will keep in an airtight container for several days.

Easy Weekend Menus

ⓦ Recipes Good for Weekdays

Beans and Vegetables

Desserts

Tips Reference

Here's an at-a-glance reference of the tips in this book. If you're ever looking for some quick info—on artichokes, for example—you can look here, instead of scanning the index and flipping through recipe pages trying to find it. The page reference leads you back to the related recipe, if you want to consult it.

Anchovies Anchovies are part of the signature flavor of Caesar salad. It doesn't taste fishy; the minced anchovies add a brininess to the seasoning, balancing the garlic, eggs, and cheese. You can leave them out, of course, but also try adding only a little at first. It may become an acquired taste. *See page 16.*

Artichokes Artichokes are available year-round, but are most plentiful and cheapest in the spring, when they're in season in the big growing areas of California. Size is irrelevant; any artichoke can be delicious, although large specimens are sometimes woody, so make sure big artichokes feel heavy for their size. Freshness, however, is important: A good artichoke will feel plump and squeak (really) when you squeeze it; the outer leaves will snap off crisply. Store refrigerated, in the vegetable bin. Use as soon as possible. *See page 90.*

I like to cut the pointed tips from artichoke leaves before cooking, but this is optional; use scissors or a heavy knife to do this. *See page 90.*

Artichokes contain an enzyme that makes them discolor as soon as they're cut and cooked; if this bothers you—it doesn't affect the flavor—drop them into a mixture of 1 tablespoon of lemon juice or vinegar per cup of water as you prepare them, and add a splash of vinegar or lemon juice to the cooking water. It's also best to use non-aluminum knives and cooking utensils when working with artichokes. *See page 90.*

Bakeware If you don't have a 10 × 2-inch round cake pan or a 10 × 2½-inch springform pan, you can make two smaller single-layer cakes with two 8 × 2-inch or 9 × 1½-inch round pans. The cakes in smaller pans will bake faster so watch that they don't burn. *See page 111.*

Beans Beans are cleaned by machines, but spend a minute or two sorting through them just before soaking or cooking: Put the beans in a pot and fill it with water, then swish the whole thing around while looking into the pot. Remove beans that are discolored, shriveled, or broken, and obviously remove any pebbles or other stray matter. *See page 24.*

After sorting through the beans, dump them into a colander and rinse for another minute. *See page 24.*

Try any of the following to vary the basic baked beans: Add Worcestershire, soy, or Tabasco sauce to taste; add an onion or two, quartered, and/or a few chunks of peeled carrots; or substitute sausage, cut into chunks, for the salt pork or bacon. *See page 86.*

Beef Because they're so tough, it's better to cook beef short ribs in liquid until they are really tender, practically mushy. Their great flavor will intensify any liquid surrounding them. *See page 74.*

Cakes When baking cakes, be sure to butter the entire pan, and flour it lightly as well. To be doubly sure you don't leave part of the delicate batter behind, it pays to line the pan with parchment or waxed paper as well. *See page 111.*

As with cookies, when you're baking cakes, rotate the pan(s) consistently to even out their baking time in hotter and cooler parts of the oven. *See page 111.*

Cakes Before you use a springform pan to bake a cake, make sure that your springform pan is watertight. (Close it and add water; as long as it doesn't leak, you're okay.) *See page 112.*

Cheesecakes Although it is not always essential, it helps to cook cheesecakes (and custards) in a water bath, which is no more than a pan of water into which you place the baking pan. By moderating the temperature around the cheesecake, the water bath (also called a bain-marie) makes for more even cooking. *See page 112.*

Chicken Years ago, chickens were labeled fryers, broilers, pullets, hens, and fowl, according to size, sex, and age. Now, you rarely see anything other than frying/broiling chickens (anything under 4 pounds or so) and roasting chickens (anything larger). "Fowl," also labeled "stewing chicken," is a large bird that is likely to be tough unless cooked in liquid; it should be quite flavorful in a dish such as Chicken in a Pot (page 64). But most commercial fowl is best used for stock. *See page 58.*

In any chicken recipe, care must be taken when cooking white and dark meat together, since white meat cooks so much faster. Sometimes, the thickness of a bone-in breast compensates for the difference, and everything finishes at about the same time. You can also increase the likelihood of even cooking by starting the legs a little before the breasts and by keeping them in the hottest part of the pan (usually the center, if you're cooking on top of the stove). *See page 60.*

It pays to cut the chicken legs in two, right through the joint where the thigh meets the lower leg to help them cook more quickly. In any case, keep an eye on things and remove the breasts as soon as they're done, even if the legs have a few minutes more to go. When measured with an instant-read thermometer, breasts are done at 160°F, thighs closer to 165°F. *See page 62.*

To reduce the messiness of spattering frying oil, I use a minimum of oil (which still seems like a lot by today's standards), and I cover the skillet for the first few minutes, which reduces spattering substantially. Then I uncover the chicken to make sure it doesn't steam in its own juices, which would defeat the point of frying—namely, a super-crisp skin and moist interior. *See page 65.*

Use a frying thermometer for frying accuracy; too-low temperatures will result in soggy chicken. As with any fried foods, the temperature will plunge as soon as you begin to add the chicken, so keep the heat as high as possible at first to enable the temperature to recover as quickly as possible. Don't crowd, either; if the chicken pieces touch each other, they won't brown at all. *See page 65.*

Collards Look for collards or kale with dark-green color and firm, unwilted leaves. Young, small leaves with stems no thicker than a pencil will be easier to clean, be less wasteful, and cook more quickly. They will also have a better texture when cooked. Collards are sold year-round, but are best in the late fall. These are sturdy greens that keep well, especially if you wrap them in plastic. They are unlikely to rot, but will begin to turn yellow after a few days; try to use them before that happens. *See page 92.*

If the stems are thick, strip the leaves, chop the stems, and start cooking the stems a couple of minutes before the leaves. *See page 92.*

Cotriade Cotriade, chowder-like stew of northern France, is traditionally made with halibut or sole, two firm-fleshed fish of the North Atlantic and North Sea. Since our sole is completely different—it's much softer—I recommend you stick to halibut. Monkfish would also be good. *See page 27.*

Couscous To give couscous real flavor—because it doesn't have a lot of flavor on its own—serve couscous with any moist stew or other dish with plenty of gravy, like Classic Osso Buco (page 75) or Lamb Stew with Potatoes (page 78). *See page 40.*

Duck "Duck" usually means Peking duck, the kind found in every supermarket. It's usually sold "fresh" but in fact is shipped frozen and then thawed; truly fresh duck is rare. All duck has dark meat that is far richer than that of chicken. *See page 66.*

To get rid of some duck fat, I've gone back to the method my mother taught me: You prick the skin as the bird roasts. It's a bit of a nuisance and sometimes makes a mess of the oven, but it works brilliantly. And, if you roast in an empty pan, you get a great deal of nice, clean fat that you can save (it keeps for weeks in the refrigerator, months in the freezer) for cooking other dishes in which you want a flavor boost. *See page 66.*

Eggplant Eggplant must be firm; like cucumber, the length is not so important, but the width is. Long, narrow eggplant tend to contain few seeds. Big, fleshy eggplant usually contain more seeds and become softer more readily. Store eggplant in the refrigerator and use it as soon as you can; although the outside will not look much different, the inside will become soft and bitter within a few days. *See page 93.*

Salting larger eggplant draws out excess moisture and a certain amount of bitterness. Trim off the ends, then cut it into slices (you can cut long slices or crosswise ones) from ½ to 1 inch thick. Or cut it into chunks. Sprinkle both sides of the slices (or all sides of the chunks) liberally with coarse salt, then let drain in a colander for at least half an hour, or up to 2 hours. Rinse and squeeze dry between paper or cloth towels. *See page 93.*

Endive All chicories, including Belgian endive, are crops of the late fall and winter and can be found when other interesting salad greens are scarce. Buy firm, fleshy specimens and store, lightly wrapped, in the vegetable bin. Belgian endive is considered best if it is nearly white; it turns green when exposed to light and becomes a little more bitter. All of these keep better than most salad greens—up to a week—but are still best when used as soon as possible. *See page 94.*

Endive, escarole, and radicchio Endive, escarole, and radicchio are done when crisp-tender; if you let them cook until they are completely tender, mushiness is the inevitable result. *See page 94.*

Fish With thicker fish fillets, those up to 1 inch or so, you can roughly estimate doneness by timing: About 8 minutes is the longest you want to cook any fillet under 1 inch thick. In addition, take a peek between the flakes of the fish; if most of the translucence is gone and the fish is tender, it's done. *See page 46.*

All food continues to cook between stove or oven and table, and fish is so delicate that fish that is fully cooked in the kitchen will likely be slightly overcooked in the dining room. *See page 46.*

Some thick fillets—striped bass, for example, or grouper—are large enough so that you can ask for a "center cut" of the fillet. Such a fillet will be of fairly even thickness from one end to the other, minimizing the differences in doneness between portions of the fish. A portion of a cod fillet can also be cut to more or less uniform thickness. *See page 47.*

Fish	Begin checking the fish after about 7 minutes of cooking time per inch of thickness. First, insert a very thin-bladed knife or skewer into the thickest part. If it penetrates with little or no resistance, the fish is done, or nearly so. *See page 47.*
Fish sauce	Nam pla—Thai fish sauce, called *nuoc mam* in Vietnam—is little more than fish, salt, and water, an ancient way of preserving fish and adding its flavor to foods long after the catch is made. It's strong-flavored (and even stronger-smelling) but a great and distinctive substitute for soy sauce. *See page 38.*
Fish steaks	Try some of these boneless fish steaks, instead of the swordfish: bluefish (delicate but strong-flavored); mako; monkfish (not a true steak, but works well in steak recipes). *See page 48.*
	Because they are of uniform thickness, or nearly so, steaks cook evenly. The problem is that some steaks—most notably swordfish and tuna—are better when they're cooked to a medium, and even a medium-rare, stage. Others, such as halibut and cod, become quite dry if they're overcooked. *See page 48.*
	Swordfish is at its most moist if you stop cooking when just a little translucence remains in the center; cook it to the well-done stage if you prefer, but get it off the heat quickly or it will be dry. Tuna is best when still red to pink in the center. Fully cooked tuna is inevitably dry. *See page 48.*
Lamb	The lamb shoulder is a cut suitable for roasting, but because of its higher fat content it is not a good grilling cut. In fact, I think its fattiness makes the shoulder (and the nearby neck) best for cooking it with liquid. And, although some people braise lamb shoulder whole, I think it makes more sense to cut it up for a stew; this makes it much easier to discard excess fat and to reduce the cooking time as well. *See page 78.*
	Lamb shoulders are sold whole or in pieces, with the bone in or out; boneless shoulders, obviously, are much easier to cut into chunks. *See page 78.*
	Discard as much of the hard lamb fat as you can when trimming lamb. *See page 78.*
Lamb shanks	Like most meats that take best to braising, lamb shanks can be cooked in advance; up to a day or two if you refrigerate them, up to a week or two if you freeze them. Skim excess fat from the top before reheating. You can braise lamb shanks on top of the stove or in the oven. *See page 80.*
Lamb stew	If there is any way you can prepare stew a day before eating it, do: The flavor will deepen, and you can skim excess fat from the surface. Lamb stew freezes perfectly, so don't worry about making it a week in advance, or about doubling the recipes. *See page 78.*
Leeks	Leeks must be washed thoroughly before use; they contain a great deal of sand. Split them in half lengthwise (they're a little easier to handle if you leave them attached at the root end for now), then rinse carefully, fanning out the layers to make sure you get every last trace of sand. Then cut off the root and chop the leeks as necessary. *See page 64.*
Lobster	There are two good ways to obtain lobster bodies for broth or soups—one is to save them from a lobster feast. The other is to get them from fish markets, which either give them away or charge only minimally. *See page 26.*

Mushrooms   Porcini (cèpes) are meaty and spectacular mushrooms. Increasingly seen fresh in this country, but still not commonly, they are always available dried, and worth keeping in your pantry. Buy from a reputable dealer in quantities of at least an ounce at a time; the small packages of ⅛ ounce for $3 are among the world's greatest rip-offs. *See page 31.*

To reconstitute dried mushrooms: Soak in hot water covered for 10 to 15 minutes or until soft. Change the water if they are not softening quickly enough, but reserve the soaking water for use in sauces, stocks, and stews (strain it first; it's often sandy). Trim the hard parts from the mushrooms and use as you would fresh. *See page 31.*

Mussels   Cleaning mussels: Farmed mussels are almost always cleaner than wild mussels and will require no more than a quick rinse and removal of the "beard," the weedy growth attached to the bottom of the shell. Wild mussels (which usually taste better) require washing in several changes of water. Discard any mussels with broken shells, those whose shells remain open after tapping them lightly, or those which seem unusually heavy—chances are they're filled with mud. As long as you do this, any mussels that don't open fully during cooking are still safe to eat; just pry apart their shells with a knife. *See page 54.*

Noodles   Use fresh Chinese egg noodles without preservatives, which are especially common in egg noodles. Use fresh noodles within 2 to 3 days of buying them, or freeze them (defrost them in the refrigerator before cooking if possible). *See page 21.*

Oil   Peanut oil works well for frying. If cost is an issue, however, use the least expensive vegetable oil you can find, such as soy or canola; as long as the oil is clean, its flavor will be neutral. *See page 65.*

Pasta   There are times when the shape of pasta matters and times when it does not. Tiny morsels, for example, such as orzo, tubetti, and ditalini, are best in soups, because they fit on a spoon. It's also true that long pastas, like spaghetti and linguine, are best with sauces that don't have large chunks in them. Sauces with chunks should be served with bigger, tube-shaped pasta, such as penne, rigatoni, or ziti, or with shells and elbows. With a sauce that is juicy with only a few chunks, you can use any pasta you like. *See page 31.*

Peppers   Yellow and orange peppers seem to be mellowest, but they're usually expensive, so red is the common first choice, green a distant last. Avoid peppers with soft spots or bruises, or those that feel very full—don't pay (by weight) for lots of seeds. Store peppers, unwrapped, in the vegetable bin, for a week or so. *See page 96.*

Peppers should always be cored and stemmed before cooking unless, of course, you're roasting or grilling them whole, as in this recipe. If you plan to cut the peppers into strips, or dice them, just start by cutting them in half; remove the cap and seed mass with your fingers. Alternatively, you can cut a circle around the cap and pull it off, along with most of the seeds; rinse out the remaining seeds. Peppers can also be peeled with a vegetable peeler, an added refinement that doesn't take long and removes an element of bitterness. *See page 96.*

Pork   Salt pork is the fat of the pig's sides and belly, simply salted to preserve it. Bacon—usually from the pig's belly—is also salted, but subsequently smoked. Both add richness to baked beans, but salt pork is usually fattier; bacon adds more flavor. (Fatback is the fresh fat from the pig's back, not salted or smoked, so it lends tenderness to meat rather than big flavor. It is often confused with salt pork and is used for foods like Breakfast Sausage, page 5.) *See page 86.*

Pork ribs Any pork ribs will work nicely in a pasta sauce; standard spareribs are great, as are the leaner (and more expensive) baby back ribs, which are cut from the loin. Country ribs are not ribs at all but a section of the loin cut into rib-like chops; they'd be fine when used for flavoring or as part of a dish, not when ribs are the focus. *See page 34.*

Potatoes Starchy potatoes, often called Idaho or Russet, make the best mashed and baked potatoes and good French fries. I call these "baking potatoes, such as Idaho or Russet." *See page 95.*

All potatoes should be quite firm when you buy them. Look out for damaged potatoes, those with mold or soft spots, those that are flabby, those with sprouts, or those with green spots. Store potatoes in a cool, dark place, but not in the refrigerator (low-starch potatoes can be refrigerated, however). Don't buy more than you can use in a month or two. *See page 95.*

Risotto Liquid must be added a bit at a time to risotto, and the heat must be kept fairly high. You must pay attention while making risotto. It doesn't require constant stirring, as some would have you believe, but neither should you leave the stove for more than a minute or so once you start the process. *See page 43.*

Do not overcook risotto. As with pasta, you should stop the cooking when there is still a tiny bit of crunch in the center of the rice kernels. *See page 43.*

Salmon Most fillets of salmon sold in supermarkets are NOT scaled. Usually that's not a problem; you can remove the skin after cooking. But here, the skin is an asset, so you may have to scale the fish yourself. Fortunately, though it's slightly messy, it's easy: Put the fish in the sink and, using an ordinary tablespoon, scrape the skin from the tail toward the head. See the scales come flying off? Keep going until they're all gone, then rinse. *See page 49.*

Sausage The best sausage contains a good deal of fat, usually about a third as much as lean. If you like, you can cut the fat to a minimum of about 20 percent of total weight, but beyond that you will be looking at a hockey puck rather than a sausage (imagine a nearly all-lean hamburger cooked until well done, and you'll have a good sense of what I'm talking about). *See page 5.*

Scallops The best scallops, depending on your wealth and geographic orientation, are either genuine bay scallops from Nantucket, Cape Cod, or Long Island, or sea scallops. (I'm going to ignore pink scallops, which are almost never seen outside of the Northwest and are not even common there.) The least desirable (and of course the least expensive), are the tiny calicos, not much bigger than pencil erasers and just as rubbery when overcooked. *See page 53.*

Many scallops are soaked in phosphates, which cause them to absorb water and lose flavor. Always buy scallops from someone you trust, and let him or her know that you want unsoaked (sometimes called "dry") scallops. *See page 53.*

Note that all scallops are sold with their tendon, a stark-white strip of gristle that attaches the muscle to the shell. It is often overlooked, and can be, especially with smaller scallops. But if you are cooking just a few scallops or have a little extra time, just strip it off with your fingers. This is an added refinement, far from essential but worthwhile. *See page 53.*

Shakes If you use berries in your fruit shake—especially raspberries and blackberries, but even strawberries—you may want to remove the seeds first. To do so, mash the berries in a bowl and then place them in a mesh strainer or sieve and press them with a wooden spoon or spatula to separate out the seeds. *See page 13.*

Shakes Sweeten a shake with sugar only to taste; bananas, for example, can sweeten other fruit enough so that sugar isn't needed at all. Use Sugar Syrup if possible: You can make it in 5 minutes and it keeps forever in the refrigerator. Alternatively, you may use honey, maple syrup, or any other sweetener. *See page 13.*

For many fruits, you'll need some added liquid in the shake as well: Use orange, apple, grape, or pineapple juice, milk, or water (sparkling water adds a nice touch). *See page 13.*

Soft-shell crabs Estimate 2 soft-shell crabs per serving for average appetites, although eating 3 or 4 is not that difficult. *See page 55.*

Have your fishmonger clean the live soft-shell crabs, then when you get them home, you can: Clean them and eat them, clean them and refrigerate them (for a day or two only), or clean them and freeze them. *See page 55.*

Soft-shell crabs spatter when fried; if you don't want to mess up the kitchen, cover them for the first 2 minutes of cooking. They will not be as crisp, but they will still be delicious and you won't regret cooking them during the 20 minutes it will take you to clean up after the meal. *See page 55.*

Spices In most homes, spices like cardamom do not get used frequently enough to be replaced often, so it's best to buy whole spices, which keep far longer than pre-ground variety. Cardamom pods can be used whole; pick them out before serving (or warn your guests to pick them out before eating). *See page 42.*

Squash Winter squash should be firm, with no soft spots or obvious damage. It's in season from late summer through winter, although it keeps so well that there are almost always some for sale. Store as you would potatoes, in a cool, dry place, but not in the refrigerator. Use within a month. *See page 97.*

The most difficult thing about winter squash is peeling it—even the smooth-skinned varieties, such as butternut, can defeat many peelers. (Use a paring knife and be careful.) For acorn and other bumpy squash, you have no choice but to cook with the skin still on. *See page 97.*

Use a cleaver or very large knife to split hard squash in half. Scoop out the seeds and strings and discard. *See page 97.*

Squash is done when very tender. If you're cooking with liquid, make sure it doesn't become waterlogged. If you're roasting or sautéing, it's difficult to overcook. *See page 97.*

Waffles The waffle iron should be hot, clean, and lightly oiled. Even some non-stick irons aren't non-stick. If your first waffles stick, next time try brushing or spraying the iron lightly with oil before turning it on. When it's preheated (most irons have indicator lights, which go off when the iron is ready), open it for a minute to let any oily smoke escape, close it until it becomes hot again, then start cooking. *See page 7.*

Don't underbake the waffles. The indicator light on many waffle irons goes on when they are still a bit underdone. They won't be crispy enough, so wait an extra minute or so after that happens. *See page 7.*

Index

Conversions, Substitutions, and Helpful Hints

Cooking at High Altitudes

Every increase in elevation brings a decrease in air pressure, which results in a lower boiling point. At 7,000 feet, for example—the altitude of many towns in the Southwest—water boils at 199°F. This means slower cooking times (and makes a pressure cooker a more desirable appliance). Families who have been living in the mountains for years have already discovered, through trial and error, the best ways to adjust.

Newcomers to high altitudes must be patient and experiment to discover what works best. But here are some general rules for high-altitude cooking:

1. For stove-top cooking, use higher heat when practical; extend cooking times as necessary. Beans and grains will require significantly more time than at sea level.

2. Assume that batters and doughs will rise faster than at sea level.

3. Over 3,000 feet, increase baking temperatures by 25 degrees.

4. Over 3,000 feet, reduce baking powder (or other leavening) measurements by about 10 percent; increase liquid in baked goods by the same percentage. You may want to reduce the amount of sugar slightly as well.

5. For every 2,000 foot increase in altitude above 3,000 feet, reduce leavening even further.

Imperial Measurements

Theoretically, both the United Kingdom and Canada use the metric system, but older recipes rely on the "imperial" measurement system, which differs from standard U.S. measurements in its liquid ("fluid") measurements:

$\frac{1}{4}$ cup = 2.5 ounces

$\frac{1}{2}$ cup ("gill") = 5 ounces

1 cup = 10 ounces

1 pint = 20 ounces

1 quart = 40 ounces

Some Useful Substitutions

1 cup cake flour = $\frac{7}{8}$ cup all-purpose flour + $\frac{1}{8}$ cup cornstarch

1 tablespoon baking powder = 2 teaspoons baking soda + 1 teaspoon cream of tartar

1 cup buttermilk = 1 scant cup milk at room temperature + 1 tablespoon white vinegar

1 cup brown sugar = 1 cup white sugar + 2 tablespoons molasses

1 cup sour cream = 1 cup yogurt (preferably full fat)

Measurement Conversions

Note that volume (i.e., cup) measures and weight (i.e., ounce) measures convert perfectly for liquids only. Solids are a different story; 1 cup of flour weighs only 4 or 5 ounces.

Dash or pinch = less than $\frac{1}{4}$ teaspoon

3 teaspoons = 1 tablespoon

2 tablespoons = 1 fluid ounce

4 tablespoons = $\frac{1}{4}$ cup = 2 fluid ounces

16 tablespoons = 1 cup = 8 fluid ounces

2 cups = 1 pint

2 pints = 1 quart

4 quarts = 1 gallon

Imperial vs. Metric

These are approximate, but are fine for all uses.

1 ounce = 28 grams

1 pound = 500 grams or $\frac{1}{2}$ kilo

2.2 pounds = 1 kilo

1 teaspoon = 5 milliliters

1 tablespoon = 15 milliliters

1 cup = $\frac{1}{4}$ liter

1 quart = 1 liter

Doneness Temperatures

Use an instant-read thermometer for the best possible accuracy; always measure with the probe in the thickest part of the meat, not touching any bone (ideally, measure in more than one place). When you gain experience in cooking, you'll be able to judge doneness by look and feel.

Beef

125°F = Rare

130–135°F = Medium-rare

135–140°F = Medium

140–150°F = Medium-well

155°F + = Well-done

Pork

137°F = Temperature at which trichinosis is killed

150°F = Slightly pink but moist

160°F = Well-done (and probably dry)

Chicken

160°F = Breast is done

165°F = Thigh is done

Lamb

125°F = Very rare

130°F = Rare

135°F = Medium-rare

140°F = Medium

150°F = Medium-well

160°F + = Well-done

USDA-Recommended Internal Temperatures

The recommended internal temperatures given in this book for meats and poultry are based on producing the best-tasting food, and are in line with traditional levels of doneness. The United States Department of Agriculture (USDA), however, generally recommends higher temperatures, which reduces the potential danger of contracting illness caused by bacteria.

Beef, Veal, and Lamb

Ground meat (hamburger, etc.) 160°F

Roasts, Steaks, and Chops

145°F = Medium-rare

160°F = Medium

170°F = Well-done

Pork (all cuts including ground)

160°F = Medium

170°F = Well-done

Poultry

Ground chicken and turkey: 165°F

Whole chicken and turkey: 180°F

Stuffing: 165°F

Poultry breasts: 170°F

Poultry thighs: Cook until juices run clear

Egg dishes: 160°F